The Betoota Advocate is a small and independent regional newspaper from far west Queensland. We pride ourselves on reporting fair and just news with an authenticity that rivals only the salt on the sunburnt earth that surrounds us here in the Queensland Channel Country.

Having been established in the mid-1800s, we are arguably Australia's oldest newspaper and have always taken pride in our ability to walk in both worlds: regional and metropolitan news. In recent times, our popularity has grown immensely as a result of a bold move to create an online revival for our publication.

Also by *The Betoota Advocate*

How Good's Australia

Australia 2020

Betoota-isms

/bəˈtutəɪzmz/ *plural noun*

1. A term used to describe the slang, lingo, nicknames and proverbs that have been either coined or featured in the writing of *The Betoota Advocate*

2. How we talk out here in the Western Queensland Channel Country

MACMILLAN
Pan Macmillan Australia

Pan Macmillan acknowledges the Traditional Custodians of country throughout Australia and their connections to lands, waters and communities. We pay our respect to Elders past and present and extend that respect to all Aboriginal and Torres Strait Islander peoples today. We honour more than sixty thousand years of storytelling, art and culture.

First published 2021 in Macmillan by Pan Macmillan Australia Pty Ltd
1 Market Street, Sydney, New South Wales, Australia, 2000

A catalogue record for this
book is available from the
National Library of Australia

Text design by Alissa Dinallo
Typeset in Mercury by Midland Typesetters, Australia
Printed by IVE

Written in partnership with the creator and writer of
The Deniliquin Dictionary, Lyndon Christie
Illustrations by Mark Chester Harding © Pan Macmillan 2021

The paper in this book is FSC® certified.
FSC® promotes environmentally responsible,
socially beneficial and economically viable
management of the world's forests.

Lady Diamantina Bowen

This book is dedicated to Queensland's founding mother, and one of the first Greeks to make the big time in Australia.

Contessa Diamantina di Roma was born in 1833 to a noble family steeped in the small aristocracy of the Venetian Ionian Islands – a British protectorate that has since been incorporated into modern-day Greece.

In April 1856, at age 22, she was married to a British colonial administrator named Sir George Bowen, an Ulster Protestant who had been posted as the political secretary of the Ionian Islands two years earlier. He was 34.

In 1859, her husband was appointed the first governor of Queensland, a colony that had just been separated from New South Wales. The couple were welcomed by over four thousand adoring Queenslanders as they stepped off the ship. She would call Queensland home for the next decade – until Sir Bowen was appointed governor-general of New Zealand.

An elegant and fascinating figure in the early days of colonial Queensland, the first lady was known for her gorgeous gardens and the Gatsby-esque dinner parties she hosted for Brisbane's burgeoning socialite class at Old Government House.

She is immortalised to this day with a bronze statue, paid for by Brisbane's Greek community, which sits outside the colonial residence that she worked so hard to instil a bit of excitement and culture into.

Queensland's first post-settlement 'power couple' retired to England in 1887 at the conclusion of Sir Bowen's final posting in the South China Sea. They had six children.

Lady Bowen remained a committed worshipper at Saint Sophia Cathedral, a Greek Orthodox Church in London, right up until her death of acute bronchitis on 17 November 1893.

Her legacy remains across Queensland with an abundance of localities named in her honour. Namely: the outback Queensland town of Roma, the Brisbane legal precinct of Roma Street, Roma Street Parklands, Ithaca Creek, Lady Bowen Hospital (now Royal Brisbane and Women's Hospital), as well as Diamantina Island off Gladstone, Mount Diamantina, the Diamantina River and, most importantly, the Diamantina Shire – home to *The Betoota Advocate*.

Her husband – who also served as a governor of Victoria, Mauritius and Hong Kong – has left a much smaller imprint on the history of Queensland. He had a dodgy inner-city Brisbane train station and few mangoes named after him.

Contents

Introduction   1

I   Pandemic Terms of Reference   2

II   The Swamp Things   12

III   Celebrity Sobriquet   26

IV   Australian Archetypes   40

V   Style & Fashion   56

VI   Dining & Cuisine   70

VII   Liquor & Gaming   82

VIII   Sports   100

        VIII – I   Sports Stars   110

IX   Town & Country   132

X   Automotive   148

XI   Geography   160

       XI – I 'The'   174

XII   Rhyming Slang   184

XIII   Betoota Proverbs   196

Index of Terms   210

Well, you're probably reading this book after someone has given it to you. Perhaps a family member, or someone you've suffered the indignation of sharing an office with. It doesn't matter. Most people who are reading this for the first time are doing so on Christmas Day, after what's been another miserable year of economic and social ruin. However, you're one of those people who, instead of just flicking through it for 30 seconds then putting it down on top of your new socks and jocks, actually takes the time to read the introduction to a book of terms (a dictionary) that *The Betoota Advocate* has either coined, adapted or outright stolen from funnier blokes than us at the pub.

That sets you apart.

It also means the editor and publisher of this book have been vindicated in their decision to include an introduction. I argued that nobody ever reads these things; that people will just palm through the book in under a minute before it's doomed to spend eternity in some suburban bathroom or some yuppie's flat-pack bookshelf. So, thank you for supporting Australian publishing.

This collection of terms and words isn't just a shrine to Australian-English, as the casual observer would deduce. They're Betoota-isms. For some reason, the Almighty God has blessed this newspaper with an enormous following in recent years – after being so cruel to it for the past century. Until *The Betoota Advocate* began publishing articles online back in 2014, it was a dying print newspaper in a thriving town on the fringe of the Simpson Desert. Many of these terms aren't new to us or anyone else who lives either in or around our beautiful medium-sized town.

So after a gun run writing articles that get read and misunderstood by people outside our town through the magic of the internet, we felt that writing and publishing this book was pertinent – if only to cement our place among the big players in the Australian media.

So enjoy this book, write your name above this body of dribble and read it cover to cover. Then give it to someone else. Because the more people who know what these terms mean, the better. The country will be richer for it. In our opinion, anyway.

Errol Parker
Editor-at-large

CHAPTER I

Pandemic Terms Of Reference

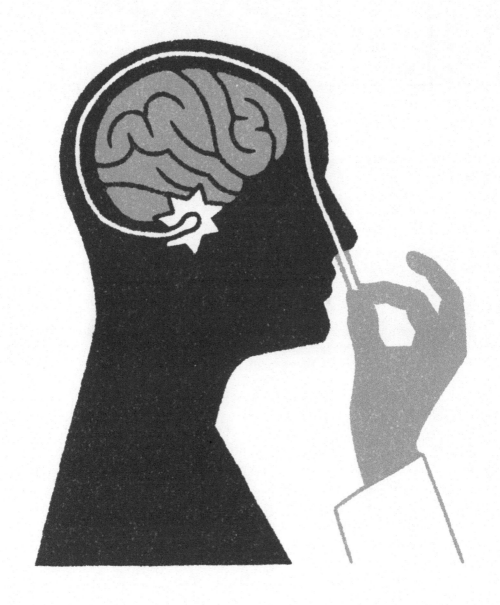

It wouldn't be a book published in this day and age without a reference to this global pandemic that has nearly stopped the world from spinning.

The Betoota-isms in this section are ones that we essentially had to come up with to make sure the articles slipped past social media censorship and weaved through complex algorithms, while also making sure that our readers were still able to decipher what it was we were trying to tell them.

Take, for example, 'AstroZucchini' – a term that *The Advocate* coined in reference to the AstraZeneca vaccine. Any mention of the major British pharmaceutical company would see our newspaper 'shadow banned' by the forces-that-be in Silicon Valley.

In short, the editors had to use the term 'AstroZucchini' in lieu of 'AstraZeneca' because of the anti-vax movement. Because this community of trust-funded linen-wearing Byron Bay mums exists, social media conglomerates like Facebook, Instagram, et al have a duty of care to prevent the spread of misinformation. You can't talk about Covid-19 on Facebook without it raising the suspicion of the AI robots that run the show there on a day-to-day level.

That translates to a loss in reach and engagement, so to find a way around it terms like 'AstroZucchini', the 'Michelle Pfeiffer' and 'The Pangolin's Kiss' came to be.

So given you know that trade secret now, I don't think this chapter needs any further introduction.

AstroZucchini

/ ˈæstroʊzuˈkini /

1. The AstraZeneca vaccine
2. A term used on social media to confuse the algorithm into thinking you're not talking about the AstraZeneca vaccine

Ex. *'Tell you what, first we shut the borders to protect the Boomers, then they refuse to take the AstroZucchini because the government scared them when they started talking about blood clots ...'*

Boomer Remover

/ ˈbumə rəˈmuvə /

1. The first wave of the coronavirus pandemic
2. The initial spread of Covid-19 that occurred February–June of 2020, resulting in a nationwide lockdown

Ex. *'When that whole Boomer Remover first flared up there was a bit of panic about the joint ...'*

Covid Coward

/ ˌkoʊvəd ˈkaʊəd /

1. An Australian expat who returned home to Australia during the Covid-19 pandemic
2. An Aussie living in London spooked by the second wave of the pandemic and variants of the virus

See also: A Sneeze Shirker

Ex. *'After doing a 15-month stint in London, Hugh got spooked and decided to return home a Covid Coward ...'*

Covid Refugee

/ ˌkoʊvəd rɛfjuˈdʒi /

1. An Australian stranded overseas during the pandemic
2. An Australian citizen unable to return home due to the lack of government support and inefficient international quarantine systems

Notable victims: Michael Slater; anyone who can't afford a first-class ticket from Heathrow or JFK

Ex. *'Did a Zoom call with Mary last night, poor girl is stuck in London as a Covid Refugee ...'*

Drive-Thru Brain Tickle

/ ˈdraɪv-θru ˈbreɪn ˌtɪkəl /

1. To be tested for the Wuhan Whooping Cough from the comfort of a motor vehicle
2. To attend a drive-through testing facility and receive a deep swabbing of the nose and throat

See also: Nasal Appraisal; Fracking the Snot-Box

Ex. *'Gary picked up runny nose in Byron over the weekend, he had to go get a Drive-Thru Brain Tickle ...'*

Glass Mask

/ glas ˈmask /
1. A schooner you hold onto in a pub or stadium to avoid having to wear a mask

See also: VIP Lanyard Lager

Ex. *'They've put in new rules at The Gabba, if ya sitting down ya gotta have a Glass Mask in ya hand at all times ...'*

Michelle Pfeiffer

/ mə ʃɛl ˈfaɪfə /

1. The Pfizer vaccine

Ex. *'I want the good vaccine, the one Scott Morrison had – the Michelle Pfeiffer ...'*

Nasal Appraisal

/ ˈneɪzəl əˈpreɪzəl /

1. To be tested for the Wuhan Whooping Cough
2. To receive a dual swab of the nose and mouth as part of a Covid-19 screening

See also: Drive-Thru Brain Tickle

Ex. *'Theresa went to Melbourne last weekend and now she's gotta go get herself a Nasal Appraisal ...'*

Pangolin's Kiss

/ pæŋˈgoʊlənz kɪs /

1. The original coronavirus (Covid-19)
2. A contagious respiratory illness caused by the SARS-CoV-2 virus

Common symptoms: Fever; dry cough; tiredness

See also: Wuhan Whooping Cough

Ex. *'Steer clear of Shane, he went to the city on the weekend and he might've picked up a case of the Pangolin's Kiss ...'*

Patagonia Parade

/ pætə‚goʊniə pə'reɪd /

1. An affluent group of walkers from Sydney's eastern suburbs, pretending to exercise
2. To put on your Lululemons, meet up with friends and participate in government-approved physical activity, disguised as socialising

See also: Puffer Shuffle; Lorna Jane Feign

Ex. *'Hugo and Yasmin laced up their Nikes and hiked the Bondi to Bronte with the rest of the Patagonia Parade ...'*

Pfizer Chief

/ 'faɪzə tʃif /

1. A person lucky enough to get the good jab
2. An individual with privilege who skips the queue and receives the Michelle Pfeiffer because they attend a prestigious private school or have political connections

See also: Queue Jumper

Ex. *'Heard William and Alex got the good jab, they go to that boater hat school so they get to be Pfizer Chiefs ...'*

Plague Enthusiast

/ 'pleɪg ɛn‚θuziəst /

1. An anti-vaxxer
2. A conspiracy theorist who thinks they know more about medical science than health experts, particularly after listening to a few very suss podcasts and following Pete Evans

See also: Anti-jabber

Ex. *'The Bowen therapist in town has been sharing some weird stuff online – she won't take a vaccine, she's a Plague Enthusiast ...'*

Scomo Showbag

/ ˈskoʊmoʊ ˈʃoʊbæg /

1. The government Coronavirus Supplement
2. Centrelink payment made to JobSeekers and JobKeepers during the Covid-19 pandemic

See also: Corona Cashola

Ex. *'Lost me job on Thursday, gotta go down to the Centrelink and line up for my Scomo Showbag ...'*

Spice Girls

/ ˈspaɪs gɜlz /

1. The people of Melbourne, because everyone is trying their hardest except Victoria
2. City of citizens continuously moving in and out of Covid-19 lockdown

Ex. *'Heard Melbourne's about to go into their sixth lockdown – when will those Spice Girls learn how to set up a proper hotel quarantine system ...'*

Sydney Sneeze

/ ˌsɪdni ˈsniz /

1. The more contagious Sydney variant of the Covid-19 virus made popular in 2021.
2. A variation of the SARS-CoV-2 virus

Common symptoms: Fever; dry cough; tiredness; attempting interstate and intrastate travel

See also: Harbour City Hack; Wentworth Wheeze

Ex: *'No way should we be opening the borders to the Southerners. They'll just bring the Sydney Sneeze up here and ruin everything.'*

Vertical Consumption

/ ˌvɜːtɪkəl kənˈsʌmpʃən /

1. To consume alcoholic beverages while standing upright
2. A beer enjoyed in the post-Covid era

See also: Upright Elbow Bend; Chair-Free Oprah Tinfrey

Ex. *'Anna has just relaxed the pub laws. Do ya wanna come down to the Schooner Shop this arvie and get around some Vertical Consumption?'*

CHAPTER II

The Swamp Things

As a presidential candidate, Donald Trump rose to prominence on the back of a promise to 'drain the swamp'.

In spite of every stupid or dangerous comment that man fired off into public debate with his chubby Twitter thumbs, it's hard to deny that 'drain the swamp' resonates with almost everyone. Especially in Australia.

From our morbidly obese rural voters who get their news from websites with hollow-point bullets somehow incorporated into the logo, to the light-rail terrace house lefties swirling their New Zealand pinot noir while reading *The Guardian* on their Androids, everyone can agree the Australian political class is about as useless as it's ever been.

To make it clear, the 'things' we're talking about are public servants. And the 'swamp' is Canberra. Or your local council chambers, or your state parliament.

To be given a nickname – whether it be a nice one or one that makes you cringe and die a bit inside whenever you hear someone say it – usually signals acceptance or at least acknowledgement from your peers. Which is very important in this country. Going it alone, especially in the bush, is a recipe for disaster.

You can tell a lot about someone by what type of nickname they have. Generally, people with a derogatory nickname aren't really respected by anyone. Like our politicians who simply lie without conscience, or our brave media identities who'd throw their own mother under a bus for a 90-character headline and an under-the-tablecloth hand job from a mining lobbyist.

These monikers don't need to be spelled out to you, but just in case they do, the next chapter should do it.

Aldi Alan

/ ˈældi ˈælən /

1. Paul Murray
2. Any conservative commentator or radio presenter, a sixth-string on-air talent unable to secure a fulltime radio show
3. A prominent shiraz conservative; low-price knock-off of Alan Jones

Famous for: Profiting from the gullibility of Boomers; pretending to care about shit

Ex. *'Went to visit Nan for afternoon tea and she had an Aldi Alan on the TV spewing out a bunch of culture wars garbage …'*

The Camperdown Frown

/ ðə ˈkæmpədaʊn fraʊn /

1. Anthony Albanese, Albo
2. Member for Grayndler, Leader of the Australian Labor Party

Famous for: Having a nickname that ends in O; supporting the Rugby League; not rocking the boat

Ex. *'I was down at the Haberfield IGA and I spotted the Camperdown Frown buying some ricotta and a box of crostoli …'*

Dictator Dan

/ ˌdɪkteɪtə ˈdæn /

1. Dan Andrews
2. Premier of Victoria and Leader of the Victorian Labor Party

Famous for: The iconic catchphrase 'Get on the beers'; being the only State Premier sponsored by North Face; being the only Premier to feature in the Triple J Hottest 100; being the only Premier to lock down an entire economy each time someone coughs on the tram

Ex. *'Apparently there's a case of Wuhan Whooping Cough in Mildura, so Dictator Dan is about to put a snap lockdown on Victoria for 14 days …'*

Double-Barrelled Brigade

/ ˌdʌbəl-ˌbærəld brəˈɡeɪd /

1. The Greens
2. Australian political party made up of woke inner-city elites, individuals with double-barrelled names e.g. Sarah Hanson-Young, Jordon Steele-John, Peter Whish-Wilson

Ex. 'My Aunt Joan has always been a bit of a greenie, she's voted for the Double-Barrelled Brigade all her life ...'

Fortunate Sons

/ ˈfɔtʃənət sʌnz /

1. The Liberal Party
2. Australian political party made up of predominately white, wealthy beta males who think they've earnt everything they have

Ex. 'Went down to watch the rugby in Bowral and the whole place was packed with Fortunate Sons ...'

Grandpa Kev

/ ˌɡrænpa ˈkɛv /

1. Kevin Rudd
2. Former Australian Labor Party politician and 26th Prime Minister of Australia
3. Mandarin-speaking politician; considered a nerd by the broad population

Famous for: Gifting every Aussie cash enough for a flatscreen plasma during the GFC; declaring war on the Murdoch media monopoly; stepping in to help accelerate our vaccine roll-out like a grandfather forced to raise his grandkids after their flaky dad goes out for some milk and smokes and never comes back

Ex. 'Remember when it was June 2021 and we still didn't have enough vaccines to immunise the under 40s even after Scotty shifted the roll-out targets six times ... Thank fuck Grandpa Kev picked up the phone to Pfizer ...'

He Who Shall Not Be Prime Minister

/ ˌhi hu ʃəl ˌnɒt bi praɪm ˈmɪnəstə /

1. Peter Dutton
2. Member for Dickson, Liberal Party politician who has held every position in the Federal Cabinet except Prime Ministership
3. Former Queensland Police officer

Famous for: An inability to count; dividing his soul into seven horcruxes pre-Liberal Party leadership spill; keeping two little girls in an offshore detention centre for their entire childhood; having a strong facial resemblance to a Desiree potato

Ex. *'Good to see He Who Shall Not Be Prime Minister has wasted another $20 million of taxpayer money on trying to send a much-loved family back to Sri Lanka ...'*

Hot Mess Gladys

/ ˌhɒt mɛs ˈglædəs /

1. Gladys Berejiklian
2. 45th Premier of New South Wales and Leader of the NSW Liberal Party, Member for Willoughby

Famous for: Spending her entire career avoiding snipes from ambitious colleagues who want her job; becoming the poster girl for bouncing back from a breakup by playing up an unlucky-in-love narrative following a highly public split with the questionable Wagga MP Daryl Maguire

Ex. *'I was in Surry Hills yesterday, swear I spotted Hot Mess Gladys going to town on a bottomless brunch with her girl gang ...'*

JohAnna

/ dʒoʊ'ænə /

1. Annastacia Palaszczuk
2. Leader of the Labor Party in Queensland and the Premier of Queensland

Famous for: Knee-jerk closing of borders during the Covid-19 pandemic; appealing to Queensland voters who used to vote for Sir Joh and love a dictator; not doing enough about the rapidly bleaching Great Barrier Reef

Ex. *'I was about to fly to Brisbane to see my wife and kids but then JohAnna decided on a whim she might shut the borders ...'*

The Kremlin

/ ðə 'krɛmlən /

1. The ABC (Australian Broadcasting Corporation) Head Office in Ultimo
2. Publicly funded national broadcaster that provides radio, television and news services to metropolitan and regional areas
3. Leftie news organisation and archenemy of *The Daily Telegraph*

Also known as: Always Broadcasting Communism; Aunty

Ex. *'Every night at 7 pm my old folks like to watch Juanita Phillips deliver the daily communist manifesto live from the Kremlin ...'*

Mad Katter

/ mæd 'kætə /

1. The Honourable Bob Katter III
2. Australian politician, Federal Member for Kennedy since 1993
3. The only man on earth capable of interrupting himself

Famous for: His hat; deranged gear changes during press conferences about gay marriage; his unquenchable thirst for the blood of saltwater crocodiles

Ex. *'Up in the Gulf, Mad Katter's been taking care of any Covid cases with a 12 gauge ...'*

Marilyn Hanson

/ ˌmɛrəlɪn ˈhænsən /

1. Pauline Hanson
2. Founder and Leader of the One Nation Party
3. Controversial Queensland politician with populist opinions on race and immigration
4. Sex icon for suburban white Boomers

Famous for: Xenophobia; making it much more difficult for women fleeing domestic violence to have their day in court; flying to the USA to ask the National Rifle Association for millions of dollars in foreign donations with the promise of eroding Australian gun laws

Ex. *'Still can't believe Marilyn Hanson wore a burqa in the Senate during Question Time. Just when you think she can't sink any lower ...'*

Mark McMao

/ ˌmak məkˈmaʊ /

1. Mark McGowan
2. Labor Premier of Western Australia and leader of a one-party state modelled on the Chinese Government
3. Former legal officer for the Australian Navy
4. State Premier regarded for his non-negotiable, cold-blooded lockdown measures during the pandemic

See also: Daddy Mark

Ex. *'Apparently Mark McMao said he'd lift the WA ban on roman orgies, but only after they have 45 days of no Covid cases ...'*

The Member for Manila

/ ðə ˌmɛmbə fɔ məˈnɪlə /

1. George Christensen
2. Member for Dawson, representing the Liberal National Party of Queensland
3. LNP backbencher notorious for spending more time in the Philippines than in his own electorate during his tenure in Parliament

Famous for: Being referred to as the 'The Fat Bachelor' by Malcolm Turnbull

Ex. *'So an obnoxiously self-righteous central Queensland bachelor spent 300 days in the Philippines on taxpayer money? No wonder they called him the Member for Manila ...'*

Paid Leave Porter

/ ˈpeɪd liv ˈpɔtə /

1. Christian Porter
2. Member for Pearce, WA, and former Attorney-General of Australia (2017–2021)
3. Australia's highest-paid stay-at-home public servant

Famous for: A mental health absence that would never be offered to his constituents in their own workplaces; other stuff that has been [redacted]

Ex. *'I spotted Paid Leave Porter down at EB Games last Tuesday buying the new Grand Theft Auto for his Playstation ...'*

The Pied Piper

/ ðə paɪd ˈpaɪpə /

1. Malcolm Turnbull
2. Former Leader of the Liberal Party and the 29th Prime Minister of Australia
3. Rhodes Scholar and former managing director of Goldman Sachs Australia

Famous for: Overseeing the legislation of same-sex marriage (2017)

Ex. *'I saw the Pied Piper from Point Piper ordering a latte at the Byron Writers Festival the other day ...'*

The RSL Tan

/ ðə ar ɛs ˌɛl ˈtæn /

1. Barnaby Joyce
2. Former Deputy Prime Minister and former Leader of the National Party, current Deputy Prime Minister and current Leader of the National Party
3. Member for New England who resembles a man 'inbred with a tomato', as described by his arch-nemesis, Hollywood actor Johnny Depp

Famous for: Threatening to put down Johnny Depp's Yorkshire terriers following a biosecurity dispute; sporting a crimson complexion caused by his undying love of cigarettes and full-strength beer

Ex. *'Most Sunday arvos you can spot The RSL Tan minesweeping schooners down at the New England Hotel ...'*

Scotty from Marketing

/ ˈskɒti frɒm ˈmakətɪŋ /

1. Scott Morrison
2. Leader of the Liberal Party and the 30th Prime Minister of Australia
3. Australia's first Pentecostal Christian Prime Minister who believes social media is the work of the devil
4. Number one ticketholder of the Cronulla Sharks

Other notable names: Scomo; The Liar from the Shire

Famous for: Shitting his pants at Engadine Maccas; having a Hawaiian holiday while the country was on fire

Ex. *'I was down in the Shire on Sunday and spotted Scotty from Marketing heading into that happy-clapper church to pray for another Sharkies premiership ...'*

Shanghai Sam

/ ʃænhaɪ ˈsæm /

1. Sam Dastyari
2. Former Australian Federal Senator, General Secretary of the New South Wales Labor Party
3. Participant in the fifth season of *I'm a Celebrity ... Get Me Out of Here!*

Famous for: Resigning from politics over his links to the Chinese Communist Party; inviting anti-halal xenophobe Pauline Hanson to Western Sydney to eat the type of food her own voters eat every time they get pissed

Ex. *'Driving home last night and I swear I heard the voice of old Shanghai Sam doing the late shift on the Ms ...'*

Tasmanian Toiga

/ tæzˈmeɪnɪən ˈtɔɪɡə /

1. Jacqui Lambie
2. Australian politician and Leader of the Jacqui Lambie Network
3. A 'lino floor feminist' who makes life hell for the Canberra political class

Famous for: A strong Tasmanian accent; keeping the bastards honest

Ex. *'Great to see a pollie with a bit of character causing strife up in the nation's capital – the Tasmanian Toiga's been sticking up for Tassie once again ...'*

The Terminator

/ ðə ˈtɜːməneɪtə /

1. Mathias Cormann
2. Former high-ranking Liberal Party politician
3. The longest-serving Minister of Finance in the history of the Australian Parliament

Famous for: Smoking cigars with Joe Hockey after slashing funding for women's shelters; having a strong Belgian-Germanic accent similar to Hollywood legend Arnold Schwarzenegger

Ex. *'Tell ya what, I really miss hearing The Terminator deliver the budget speech. That accent somehow softens the blow of realising I'll never own a house ...'*

Uncle Tony X

/ ˌʌŋkəl ˈtoʊni ɛks /

1. Tony Abbott
2. Former Leader of the Liberal Party and the 28th Prime Minister of Australia
3. Member for Warringah and prominent Northern Beaches elder

Famous for: Being the prime minister for just short of the two years required to become eligible for a lifelong pension; making very powerful enemies out of every woman in Sydney's North Shore; finishing his career as 'the special envoy on Indigenous affairs' – a role created by Scott Morrison that sent him to remote parts of Australia and away from the media

Ex. *'Heard Uncle Tony X is set to play halfback for Walgett in the Koori Knockout this weekend ...'*

CHAPTER III

Celebrity Sobriquet

Because we are a people largely devoid of culture, Australians cling to their celebrities like a swarm of eels slowly eating a pigeon that accidentally found itself drowning in a park pond.

It's not a bad thing, it's just what happens to a nation when your history books basically start at Captain Cook's arrival and then fast-forward to the Sydney Olympics, stopping only for that war we lost in Turkey.

There's something innate within all Australians that prevents us calling something by what other English-speaking people would call it. Why give something that doesn't need a new name a new name? Because why not. We aren't in England.

If you become famous in this country, whether it be for shooting people or scoring a lot of points in some kind of sports match, odds are you'll get a nickname.

We are a complex people. While on one hand we idolise people like Ned Kelly, on the other we phone the police whenever we think a group of old papous are breaking lockdown rules by playing a game of cards past curfew. We love our celebrities and we love humanising them with overly familiar bynames, but it's hard to tell if these are a badge of honour or a black mark. It's certainly not as clear-cut as Bruce Springsteen being called The Boss, or Beyoncé being called Queen.

Some of these sobriquets (which means nickname, by the way) are complex and others are just crude.

Like Australians.

Acca Dacca

/ ˈækə ˈdækə /

1. AC/DC
2. Legendary Australian hard rock band, formed in Sydney in 1973 by Satan's sons Malcolm and Angus Young

Notable hits: 'Highway to Hell' (1979); 'Back in Black' (1980); 'Thunderstruck' (1990)

Ex. *'Come round this arvie – I put new speakers in the Commodore, gonna test 'em out with some Acca Dacca …'*

That Bald Prick

/ ðæt ˈbɔld prɪk /

1. Kochie; David Koch
2. Australian breakfast TV presenter and ambulance chaser
3. Chairman of the Port Adelaide Football Club

Famous for: Having the chromest dome to grace our television screens; talking over the top of the people he's interviewing

Ex. *'Switched on the TV to check out the weather and That Bald Prick was yapping about finance or something again …'*

The Baroness of Broadbeach

/ ðə ˈbærənɛs əv ˈbrɔdbitʃ /

1. Sophie Monk
2. Australian media personality, singer and TV presenter
3. Former school captain of MacGregor State High School, Queensland

Famous for: Being a founding member of Australian girl group Bardot; appearing on *The Bachelorette* (Season 3, 2017)

Ex. *'Tell ya what, if the Gold Coast host the Olympics one day it'd be beaut to see the Baroness of Broadbeach light the cauldron …'*

The Boozy Balkan

/ ðə ˌbuzi ˈbɔlkən /

1. Karl Stefanovic
2. Australian television presenter, longstanding co-host of the breakfast program *Today* (Nine Network)
3. Gold Logie winner for Most Popular Personality (2011)

Famous for: Hosting breakfast television while intoxicated after the 2009 Logie Awards; being a one-eyed Queenslander

Ex. *'I was at the airport in Rocky and I swear I spotted the Boozy Balkan knocking back a Milton Mango in the Qantas lounge ...'*

The Christmas Cake

/ ðə ˈkrɪsməs ˌkeɪk /

1. Delta Goodrem
2. Australian singer and songwriter
3. Cryonically preserved between seasons of *The Voice* by Channel Nine executives

Famous for: Making an appearance once a year

Ex. *'Every time the carols are on TV Dad won't turn it off until The Christmas Cake and Olivia Newton-John do their duet ...'*

Caboolture Crooner

/ kəˈbʌltʃə ˌkrunə /

1. Keith Urban
2. Kiwi-born, Queensland-raised, Grammy Award–winning country music star
3. Possibly the only Order of Australia recipient to rock a flavour saver

Famous for: Being a sex icon for rural mothers; being married to Australian actor Nicole Kidman

Ex. *'Glad that Nickers dropped that Tom Cruise fella, I reckon almost everyone would much prefer to hang out with the Caboolture Crooner ...'*

The Duchess of Dalby

/ ðə ˈdʌtʃɛs əv ˈdɒlbi /

1. Margot Robbie
2. Internationally acclaimed Australian actor, born on the dust plains of the Darling Downs, Queensland
3. Actor nominated for Academy Awards for performances in *I, Tonya* (2017) and *Bombshell* (2019)

Famous for: Being on *Neighbours*

Ex. *'Walkin' through the newsagency yesty and spotted the Duchess of Dalby on the front cover of* Vogue *...'*

Everywhere Eddie

/ ˈɛvriwɛə ˌɛdi /

1. Eddie McGuire
2. Australian media personality, radio host, TV presenter
3. Former president of the Collingwood Football Club

Famous for: Hosting *Who Wants to Be a Millionaire?*, *Millionaire Hot Seat*, *The Footy Show* (AFL), Commonwealth Games (1998), Australian Formula 1 Grand Prix (1998), Logie Awards (2003, 2004 2005), *1 vs. 100*, *A Current Affair*, *The Million Dollar Drop*, *Between the Lines*, *This is Your Life*, Fox Footy, Triple M's *Hot Breakfast* (radio)

Ex. *'There's three things in life you can guarantee. Death. Taxes. And that Everywhere Eddie will be on TV tonight ...'*

The Final Word

/ ðə ˈfaɪnəl wɜd /

1. Gina Rinehart
2. Mining magnate, Australia's richest individual with an estimated net worth of $36 billion as of 2021
3. Australia's largest landholder, controlling 1.2% of the entire country's landmass

Famous for: Being filthy stinking rich; teaching Chinese businessmen how to push cattle at the Shanghai Equestrian School

Ex. *'Good to see they approved another iron ore pit in the Pilbara, guessing the Final Word made a few calls to Parliament ...'*

The Finger

/ ðə'fɪŋgə /

1. Powderfinger
2. Iconic Queensland rock band fronted by 'The Toowong Troubadour', Bernard Fanning
3. Early pioneers of 2000's 'Briscore' movement

Notable hits: 'My Happiness' (2000); '(Baby I've Got You) On My Mind' (2003); 'Sunsets' (2003)

Ex. *'Did you hear they're gonna dye the Brown Snake maroon this weekend to celebrate The Finger getting back together …'*

The Foil Packet Chef

/ ðə 'fɔɪl ˌpækət 'ʃɛf /

1. Pete Evans
2. Australian chef, TV presenter and conspiracy theorist
3. Former judge on Channel 7's *My Kitchen Rules*

Famous for: Promoting tin foil conspiracy theories and the use of alternative medicines; spreading anti-vaxxer beliefs with no scientific basis

See also: Plague Enthusiast

Ex. *'My Aunt Wendy has been posting some weird shit on Facebook, I think she might be reading a bit too much garbage from the Foil Packet Chef…'*

The Fun Freezer

/ ðə 'fʌn ˌfrizə /

1. Scott Pape, 'The Barefoot Investor'
2. Australian author of the bestselling financial self-help books *The Barefoot Investor* (2016) and *The Barefoot Investor for Families* (2018)
3. Sunraysia's Golden Son and leader of the ING Cult

Famous for: Ruining everything that brings joy in life; signing every Australian up to an Orange ING Bank card; some shit about buckets

Ex. *'I used to join my workmates for a pub schnitzel every Friday, but after reading that book by the Fun Freezer I just sit and chew on leftovers …'*

The Gun

/ ðə ˈɡʌn /

1. Leigh Sales
2. Australian journalist and author, host of ABC's current affairs program *7.30*
3. Walkley Award–winning journalist and Member of the Order of Australia

Famous for: Interviewing every living Australian prime minister; terrifying every living Australian prime minister

Ex. *'God, it was good to see The Gun tear Scomo to shreds last night on 7.30 …'*

Keith's Arrow

/ ˈkiθs ˌærəʊ /

1. Nicole Kidman, because she keeps Keith on the straight and narrow
2. Academy Award–winning Australian actor who grew up in Lane Cove, Sydney
3. Goodwill Ambassador for the United Nations Development Fund for Women
4. Married to the 'Caboolture Crooner', country music star Keith Urban

Famous for: Appearing in award-winning films such as *The Hours* (2002), *Australia* (2008), *Lion* (2016)

Ex. *'I was up in Tamworth for the Country Music Festival, swear I spotted Keith's Arrow up the front cheering on her fella …'*

The Koori Rose

/ ðə ˈkʊri roʊz /

1. Brooke Boney
2. Australian journalist, entertainment reporter for *Today* (Nine Network) and former Triple J newsreader
3. Gamilaroi woman from Muswellbrook, NSW

Famous for: Becoming the first Indigenous Australian woman to host a breakfast television program in Australia; beginning news segments with 'Yaama', the traditional greeting of the Gamilaroi people

Ex. *'I saw the Koori Rose at the Logies, has she got a man or what?'*

The Neutron Bomb

/ ðə ˈnjutrɒn bɒm /

1. Olivia Newton-John
2. British-Australian singer, actor, entrepreneur and four-time Grammy Award winner
3. Officially recognised as a national living treasure by the National Trust of Australia

Famous for: Playing the role of Sandra 'Sandy' Olsson in the 1978 musical adaption of *Grease*

Ex. *'Grease came on the TV last night and I swear my old man still has the hots for the Neutron Bomb ...'*

The News

/ ðə ˈnjuz /

1. Kay McGrath
2. Australian journalist, TV presenter for Seven News Brisbane
3. Recipient of an Order of Australia in recognition of her work in media and child protection

Famous for: Being the most trusted journalist north of the Tweed

Ex. *'There's only one TV anchor Mum and Dad trust and that's The News ...'*

Our Geoffrey

/ ˈaʊə ˌdʒɛfri /

1. Geoffrey Rush
2. Award-winning Australian actor, one of the few living artists to receive a Triple Crown (an Oscar, a Tony and an Emmy)
3. Australian of the Year in 2012
4. The inner-city lefties' problem child

Famous for: Taking News Corp to the cleaners; causing theatre-crowd Boomers to decide they'd had enough of the #MeToo movement

Ex. *'Our Geoffrey's a national treasure and shouldn't be treated like an uncouth tradie or NRL player. He's just a playful thespian ...'*

The Pymble Pirate

/ ðə ˌpɪmbəl ˈpaɪrət /

1. Peter FitzSimons
2. Australian author, journalist and media personality

Famous for: Wearing a red bandana; elitism

Ex. *'Didn't know what to get my old Uncle Kev for Christmas so I got him one of those war books by The Pymble Pirate ...'*

The Rusty Rabbit

/ ðə ˈrʌsti ˌræbət /

1. Russell Crowe
2. Academy Award–winning actor in *Gladiator* (2000) and Golden Globe Award winner for Best Actor in *A Beautiful Mind* (2001)
3. Co-owner of the South Sydney Rabbitohs

Famous for: Featuring on the photo wall of every Italian restaurant in Australia; throwing phones and fightin' round the world

Ex. *'I was at the footy and spotted The Rusty Rabbit up there in the box with half of the Avengers and one of the Burgess boys ...'*

Silverhair

/ ˈsɪlvəhɛə /

1. the name for the middle-aged rock gods formerly known as Silverchair
2. Generation-X Australian rock band from Newcastle, NSW, fronted by Daniel Johns

Famous for: Mid-nineties success off the back of the global grunge movement; being your uncle's go-to CD after a few Tooheys

Ex. *'Was driving up the Pacific, and as soon as I got to Hexham the radio started spurting out nothing but Silverhair ...'*

The Stunner from Gunner

/ ðə ˈstʌnə frəm ˈɡʌnə /

1. Miranda Kerr
2. Famous Australian model and businesswoman
3. Married to billionaire Snapchat CEO Evan Spiegel; previously married to *Lord of the Rings* elf Legolas (Orlando Bloom)

Famous for: being Australia's first Victoria's Secret model; being raised in Gunnedah, NSW

Ex. *'I was having a schooner down at the Courty and our hometown girl, the Stunner from Gunner, was on the TV ...'*

Talisman of the Top End

/ ˈtæləzmən əv ðə tɒp ˈɛnd /

1. Jessica Mauboy
2. ARIA Award–winning Australian singer and actor, born and raised in Darwin
3. Runner-up of the 2006 season of *Australian Idol*

Famous for: Being the pride of Darwin; starring in films such as *Bran Nue Dae* (2010) and *The Sapphires* (2012)

Ex. *'Did you know the Talisman of the Top End once toured with Beyoncé? Or should I say Beyoncé toured with her?!'*

The Trophy Hunter

/ ðə ˈtroʊfi ˌhʌntə /

1. Baz Luhrmann
2. Decorated Australian filmmaker and producer

Famous for: The Red Curtain Trilogy, a trio of films including *Strictly Ballroom* (1992), *Romeo + Juliet* (1996) and *Moulin Rouge!* (2001)

Ex. *'Still waiting for The Trophy Hunter to release his new Elvis film, I think he'll clean up in Oscar season …'*

Town Crier

/ taʊn ˈkraɪə /

1. Joe Hildebrand
2. Australian journalist, TV and radio presenter

See also: The Tele Bellman

Ex. *'As if being stuck in traffic isn't bad enough, had to listen to the Town Crier on 2GB rabble on about some shit about university bathroom signs …'*

The Whistle

/ ðə ˈwɪsəl /

1. Julian Assange
2. Townsville-born computer programmer, activist and author; founder of international whistleblowing platform WikiLeaks
3. *Time*'s 2010 Person of the Year (Readers' Choice)

Famous for: being Australian Indoor Cricket Captain (Tour of London 2012–2019); being former Townsville Crocs' number one ticketholder; destabilising multiple national governments and disrupting international law and order

Ex. *'Did you see that WikiLeaks already revealed the winner of the Triple J Hottest 100? The Whistle has been up to his shifty little tricks again …'*

The Wick Wilkins

/ ðə wɪk ˈwɪlkənz /

1. Richard 'Dickie' Wilkins
2. New Zealand-Australian television and radio presenter
3. Animatronic robot built by Channel Nine to host Marvel film red carpet events and update the nation on who Zac Efron is shaggin'

Famous for: His eternal youth; his eternal wick

Ex. *'Turned on the telly and The Wick Wilkins was doing a live cross from the Grammys ... he's bringing back the frosted tips ...'*

CHAPTER IV

Australian Archetypes

If you thought we only gave nicknames to public servants, celebrities and our friends, then you would be wrong. Australians also give nicknames to people they don't know – sometimes even people they actively despise.

Take real estate agents and their lesser siblings, leasing agents. Rather than referring to them by their hard-earned job title, people around town started to call them AirPods with Legs when those terrible, pretentious Apple headphones were first set upon this unsuspecting country like a Spitfire barrel-rolling out of a billowing cumulus and into a formation of Messerschmitts.

That name stuck, and it's become the go-to term in Betoota whenever someone has to interact with a real estate agent.

In the suburbs and towns across Australia the same stereotypes exist everywhere, be they in education, beauty, construction or hospitality. The preferred sports sometimes change between towns, but that's about it. Same language, same class structure, same rapid departure from religion, same energy drinks on special at the servo.

Apart from that thin stretch of coastline between the Gold Coast and Lismore, there are very few towns in Australia where everyone drives a nice car.

An archetype is a very typical example of a certain person, which, come to think of it, is a pretty good definition of a real estate agent on its own.

The Betoota Advocate, believe it or not, takes a rather dim view of the johnny-come-latelys who have turned to making a quid out of manipulating the property market into this hysterical bubble we find ourselves in. That's a subject for a different time, though; perhaps we'll write a book about them one day that our publisher will laugh at in the early stages and try to steer us away from.

But there are plenty of other types of Australians out there that we talk about, or write about in *The Betoota Advocate* newsroom.

The Australians in this section are not famous, and they are not public servants.

They're just like you and me.

Adult Babysitter

/ əˈdʌlt ˈbeɪbɪsɪtə /

1. A personal trainer
2. A lycra-clad, gym-dwelling individual who yells at adults and posts selfies for a living
3. Official career path of the high school sports captain

See also: Roid Muncher; Botox with Legs; Professional Push-up Counter

Ex. *'Nothing ruins a nice walk in the park like an Adult Babysitter counting squats over a UE BoomBox ...'*

AirPod with Legs

/ ˈɛəpɒd wɪθ lɛgz /

1. A real estate agent
2. A talentless property pusher who specialises in opening doors and handing out business cards

Key identifiers: Pocket square; leased BMW; concreted quiff; flammable Tarocash suit

See also: Property Peddler; A Door Opener

Ex. *'Went to an auction on Sat'dee, almost fainted from the hair gel fumes coming from the AirPod with Legs ...'*

Art Gallery Valerie

/ ˈat ˌɡæləri ˈvæləri /

1. Regional fine art connoisseur and owner of the Betoota tourist gift shop
2. Committee member (twice curator) of the Betoota Old and New Art (BONA) Gallery

Enjoys: Applying for government arts grants; Richard Glover; being the only person in town who's been to Dark Mofo

Key identifiers: Long free-flowing clothing purchased at Brisbane's West End markets; several bangles on each arm; a short spiked crop inspired by Lee Lin Chin, usually dyed purple

Ex. *'Got stuck talkin' to Art Gallery Valerie at the farmers market, she's trying to convince me to model for the naked life drawing class ...'*

BCF Jeff

/ bi si ˌɛf ˈdʒɛf /

1. Hardened male; skilled tradesperson with outdoor hobbies and a deep interest in horse and greyhound racing
2. More intimidating form of Brian, smarter than a Keith, not as violent as a Tyson

Notable skills: plumbing; quoting trade jobs; collecting car parts; executing U-turns at intersections

Enjoys: Talking with arms folded; 3/4 length board shorts; thongs; Facebook Marketplace

Ex. *'Mate, if you need a hand fitting out your 4x4 give BCF Jeff a call, his ute has all the fruit ...'*

The Beep Tester

/ ðə ˈbip ˌtɛstə /

1. A high school Physical Education teacher
2. A Year 7–10 PE teacher who teaches Bullrush and enjoys saying, 'Oi!!'
3. Official career path of the high school cross-country winner, fringe NRL prodigy

Key traits: Wears Asics running shoes with Tarocash suit pants; drives a Mazda CX-5; receding hairline

Ex. *'Fuck, I copped a Friday detention from the Beep Tester for not wearin' my sports uniform again …'*

Bean Counter

/ ˈbin ˌkaʊntə /

1. A tax accountant
2. A white collar professional who records, tallies and analyses financial numbers
3. A corporate drone devoid of personality, often in training for a triathlon or long-distance fun run

Enjoys: Coldplay; competing in endurance sports; paying $16 for a curried egg sandwich and a Vitamin water

Ex. *'Got stuck talking to my cousin's new boyfriend, Daniel, at the family Christmas, he's a Bean Counter from the city and about as fun as a shark attack …'*

Becky

/ ˈbɛki /

1. A privileged white feminist unaware of their own position of privilege
2. An upper middle class, pick-and-choose progressive who cluelessly participates in casual racism and classism

Ex. *'I used to love reading the university feminist society newsletter, but they kind of revealed themselves to be a big bunch of Beckys during the Black Lives Matters protests …'*

The Blue Bloods

/ ðə ˈblu blʌdz /

1. The rich snobs in town
2. Betoota's snotty bourgeoise Liberal voters who maintain a polo stick's length distance from the local community for fear of blue-collar workers and public schools
3. A portion of the population who don't seem to work

Key traits: Drive Audi Q7s; send children to boarding school down the road, from Year 7; puffer vest enthusiasts

Ex. *'Took the kids up to Snob Hill to check out the Christmas lights, those Blue Bloods always have the best lights in town ...'*

Bush Uce

/ ˈbʊʃ jus /

1. A person of Pacific Island heritage growing up in a country town
2. A Polynesian living in rural Australia

Notable skills: Touch football; singing R&B renditions of Eric Clapton

Ex. *'The Betoota Muttaburrasaurus side is looking real good, that new centre, Sione, has brought a bunch of his Bush Uce mates to come play ...'*

Busted Cocky

/ ˌbʌstəd ˈkɒki /

1. A bankrupt farmer
2. A farmer in a difficult financial situation due to drought, flood, a once-in-a-generation mice plague with a lack of support from local, state and federal government

See also: A Bushie

Ex. *'My Uncle Greg is the last Busted Cocky in our family, owns a couple hundred acres down in Narrabri ...'*

Colourful Racing Identity

/ ˈkʌləfəl ˈreɪsɪŋ aɪˈdɛntəti /

1. A euphemism for a person believed to be involved in criminal activity
2. A term used by journalists to avoid defamation by individuals connected to organised crime and government corruption
3. A character associated with horse racing and/or corrupt local councils (see also: The Trough)

See also: Kings Cross Socialite

Ex. *'I was in the Members at Rosehill Races on Saturday and I bumped shoulders with a couple of Colourful Racing Identities ...'*

Concrete Cowboy

/ ˈkɒnkrit ˈkaʊbɔɪ /

1. Inner-city business professional who pounds the pavement in R.M. Williams, a gingham check shirt and a puffer vest
2. A man who has never actually ridden a horse, but dresses as though he does it for work

Enjoys: Range Rovers; weekends in Bowral/Berry/Double Bay/Stanthorpe/Mooloolaba; every country race meet in outback towns that aren't too rough

See also: Pitt Street Farmer, Queens Street Ringer

Ex. *'Almost got T-boned yesterday by a Concrete Cowboy running a red light in an X5 ...'*

Country Town Cardashian

/ kʌntri ˈtaʊn kaˈdæʃiən /

1. Regional hairdresser or beautician
2. A local girl with expert up-to-date knowledge of the latest small-town gossip and drama
3. An apprentice at the Rumour Mill (hairdressing salon)

Key identifiers: Drives a Suzuki Swift; butterfly tattoo; wears ugg boots March–November

Enjoys: UDLs; watching *Married at First Sight*; local gossip

Ex. *'The misso likes to go to Allure Hair & Beauty for a cut 'n' dry, the Country Town Cardashian down there knows all the good oil ...'*

Devil Dodger

/ ˈdɛvəl ˈdɒdʒə /

1. A extremely devout Christian, driven to faith by fear of the devil
2. A sanctimonious old-school Christian who attends a church service more than once a week

See also: Satan Shunner; Concrete Catholic

Ex. *'We're having Jack's funeral down at St Luke's Cathedral. Poor bloke never wanted a church funeral but apparently his mum's a real Devil Dodger ...'*

DINKs

/ dɪŋks /

1. Acronym for Double Income No Kids
2. A wealthy, often gay, couple with no children
3. A lucrative target demographic for the marketing of luxury brands, holidays and fashion

Ex. *'Love when Auntie Joan and Auntie Jan come to Christmas, they always get me the best presents and come steaming in with a real DINK energy ...'*

Hydraulic

/ haɪˈdrɒlɪk /

1. Someone who will steal (lift) anything
2. A light-fingered thief who will pocket anything shiny that catches their eye

See also: Penny Prigger

Ex. *'Keep an eye on Caleb's brother, that shifty little prick is a bit of a Hydraulic ...'*

Irish Twins

/ ˌaɪrɪʃ ˈtwɪnz /

1. Male siblings born less than twelve months apart
2. Local scallywags, often suspended or caught skipping school
3. Rhyming names e.g. Cayden & Jaiden, Daxton & Ashton

Enjoy: Throwing rocks at trains; Xbox; Cheese and Bacon Shapes; drinking out of the tap in other people's backyards

Ex. *'I was driving through town and spotted those Irish Twins from Betoota Ponds peggin' chicken nuggets at kids at the skatepark ...'*

Juke Box

/ ˈdʒuk bɒks /

1. Local footy player who puts on the big hits
2. A reserve grade Rugby League or Rugby Union player who only participates in weekend sport for the sake of ironing blokes out
3. A socks-down, bootlaces-taped type operator

Famous alumni: Steve Matai; Sonny Bill Williams; Nigel Plum, Sam Burgess

Ex. *'Went down to watch the rugby and no wonder they call Harry the Juke Box – that bloke does nothing but put on the big hits ...'*

Karen

/ ˈkærən /

1. An entitled, white middle-class woman displaying obnoxious behaviour in public, particularly towards retail employees
2. A pejorative term used to profile a deep-Gen-X or shallow-Boomer woman who carries a sense of entitlement beyond the scope of what is normal

Key identifiers: A 'Karen' bob (an inverted lob, short, angled and layered with streaks or highlights); P!nk tickets; colour matching lippy and jewellery

Ex. *'Took me an age to check into my flight, there was a Karen making an absolute scene at the front desk about missing out on the exit row ...'*

Kawasaki King

/ kawəˈsaki kɪŋ /

1. Hot-headed rural male with a penchant for fangin' dirt bikes and energy drinks

Key identifiers: SS Commodore ute; Jetpilot boardshorts; rat's tail; Southern Cross tattoo

Enjoys: Diesel fumes; Guava Vodka Cruisers; doing a 'Shoey'; Facebook fights with 'dog cunts'

Notable names: Cody/Khodii, Tyson, Nathan

Ex. *'Did ya hear about Tyson the Kawasaki King? Just got done by the coppers for cutting hoops in the Macca's carpark ...'*

Lightning

/ ˈlaɪtnɪŋ /

1. A woodchopper who can't strike the same place twice
2. A labourer that aims like a cross-eyed magpie

See also: Specsaver Labourer

Ex. *'Went camping with Robbo, no wonder they call him Lightning. That fella couldn't split a Maxibon in half …'*

Linenfluencer

/ ˈlɪnənfluənsə /

1. An earthy beige-linen-clad influencer residing in Byron Bay
2. A city yuppie who's participated in the great white migration from North Bondi to Byron Bay
3. A Venroy-wearing e-commerce professional

Enjoys: long lunches at Wategos; naming their children 'Atticus' or 'Juniper'

Ex. *'Went up to the Northern Shivers last weekend, whole place was chockas with Linenfluencers protesting about the 5G towers …'*

London Fog

/ ˈlʌndən fɒg /

1. A lazy construction worker who never lifts
2. A lethargic tradie who never gets stuck into hard labour

See also: A Blister (turns up when the work's done)

Ex. *'Took me three hours to load the truck this arvie cos I was partnered up with Craig. God, that bloke's a London Fog …'*

SOCK

/ sɒk /

1. An acronym for Some Other Cunt's Kid
2. Term used by the friends of a person currently managing children that are not biologically theirs

Ex. *'Yeah, Daz can't come to the pub, he's gotta take his new girlfriend and the SOCK out to the movies tonight …'*

Scientologist

/ saɪˈnɒlədʒəst /

1. A chiropractor
2. A health professional trained in the treatment and mobilisation of the musculoskeletal system
3. An incredibly expensive pseudoscientific alternative physical therapy marketed as a pyramid scheme

Ex. *'As part of my worker's compo insurance, I've gotta go visit the Scientologist and get treated with that woo woo medicine …'*

Swing Voter

/ swɪŋ ˈvoʊtə /

1. Suburban mum of three or more children who drives a Kia Carnival and manages the school canteen
2. Less aggressive form of Karen who will, however, raise issues via email, Facebook comments and phone calls to the school principal

Notable skills: Hairdressing; netball coaching; voicing concerns; shopping weekly specials at Aldi

Enjoys: Cab sav; Pandora bracelets; Shania Twain; Gold Coast holidays

Ex. *'This* Daily Mail *article about Bindi Irwin is going off, all the Swing Voters are throwing their two cents in …'*

Terry Tough Cunt

/ ˌtɛri ˈtʌf kʌnt /

1. Highly strung male eager to display physical toughness and macho tendencies
2. Patronising term used to identify unnecessarily aggressive male behaviour

Enjoys: Tailgating; servo pies; Super Cheap Auto

Dislikes: domestic animals that don't serve the purpose of intimidating; real estate agents; salad; the mayor

See also: Hardcore Harry; Chainsaw

Ex. *'Almost had a bust-up at the lights this morning, this Terry Tough Cunt in a HiLux was riding me up the arse ...'*

Three One

/ ðə θri ˈwʌn /

1. A FIFO worker, fly-in fly-out tradesperson
2. A mining worker on a 'three weeks on / one week off' roster

Key traits: Wears hi-vis shirts; suffers from a crippling mobile gambling addiction; owns a Ford Raptor; jetski enthusiast

See also: Pilbara Professional

Ex. *'Ever since Kane became a Three One, that bloke's been pissing a tonne of cash up the wall every time he comes back to town ...'*

Trustafarian

/ trʌstəˈfɛəriən /

1. A young, wealthy white millennial who adopts a neo-hippie alternative lifestyle
2. A spoiled rich kid who embraces anti-Western counterculture, financially backed by their parents' trust fund

Key identifiers: Harem pants; a nose piercing; enthusiasm for South East Asian backpacking, bongo circles and anti-vaccination protests

Natural habitats: Byron Bay; Chiang Mai (Thailand); Vang Vieng (Laos)

Ex. *'Went up to Byron for a holiday and the whole place was overrun with Trustafarians busking with their pan flutes ...'*

Tupperware Christian

/ ˈtʌpəwɛə ˈkrɪstʃən /

1. New Age Christian, associated with Hillsong (aggressive Pentecostal megachurch)
2. Resides in the Bible belt of Sydney known as 'The Hills'

Enjoys: Fedora hats; chinstrap beards; acoustic singalongs; praising Jesus in a leather jacket

See also: Bible Basher; God Squad; Happy Clapper

Ex. *'No wonder Elijah is so friendly, he's one of those Tupperware Christians from The Hills ...'*

CHAPTER V

Style &
Fashion

One thing that is certain in this life is that you are always going to have at least one uncle who turns up to a funeral wearing a fedora.

Maybe it's the divorce, maybe it's his newfound love of jazz. Whatever it is, it's directly related to a mid-life crisis.

And what better way of letting your community know where you are at in life than through the ancient forms of self-expression known as style and fashion.

Whether it's subconscious or not, we can tell a lot through fashion.

We can spot an undercover cop when we see a Hawaiian shirt and cargo shorts on a 40-year-old with suspiciously large biceps.

We can tell we are about to be relieved of our mobile phone when we see the Nautica cap and the Gucci bumbag on a teenager at the train station.

When we see an elderly Italian woman wearing all black, we can assume she has been widowed at some point over the last four decades.

We know when someone's made the big time, because they start rocking a gold airport watch or a tropical kaftan that could blind Ken Done.

The fact is, Australians know fashion better than anyone – we just don't talk about it.

The following chapter should reaffirm everything you've ever thought about the clothes, accessories and hairstyles of everyone around you. We've simply put it in print.

Bali Bonds

/ 'bali bɒndz /

1. A Bintang singlet
2. A counterfeit singlet purchased by an Australian tourist while holidaying in Indonesia

Ex. 'You can tell Brad spends a bit of time in Kuta. The bloke loves a sun-tanning holiday, drinking cheap grog in his Bali Bonds ...'

Bolt-Ons

/ 'boʊlt-ɒnz /

1. A set of breast implants
2. To receive breast enlargement surgery for aesthetic purposes
3. Common procedure undertaken by reality TV contestants to increase their chances of appearing in a *Daily Mail* article
4. Official cosmetic surgery of the 30+ recently divorced cougar

See also: Gold Coast Headlights

Ex. 'Have you seen Cindy lately? Gotta be bolt-ons, right?'

Boon Broom

/ 'bun brum /

1. A overtly masculine moustache
2. The growth of dense facial hair on the upper lip

See also: Wally Lewis Lip Rug; Froth Filter

Ex. 'Mate, ya gotta throw Ben some dollars for his Movember efforts, his Boon Broom is looking fantastic ...'

Byron Nappy

/ ˈbaɪrən ˌnæpi /

1. A pair of Afghan pants or harem pants
2. Loose-fitting hippie pants worn by Northern Rivers locals while participating in a drum circle or slide guitar busking

See also: Nimbin Chinos

Ex. *'Molly went up to BluesFest and by Day Two she had bought herself a Byron Nappy from the hemp markets ...'*

Choppercore

/ ˈtʃɒpəkɔ /

1. A fashion style paraded by inner-city creatives and university hipsters, consisting of a white T-shirt tucked into stretch jeans, paired with Blundstone boots
2. A vintage streetwear style reminiscent of paroled 1990s underworld figures

Ex. *'Went to the big smoke to see a DMAs show and the whole of Enmore Theatre was filled with fellas in their Choppercore ...'*

Coota Suit

/ ˈkutə sut /

1. A double denim outfit consisting of stonewash blue jeans paired with a matching denim jacket/shirt
2. Sunday church wear of the Happy Clapper or Tupperware Christian

Variations: Texas Tuxedo, as above plus cowboy hat and boots

Notable example: Britney Spears and Justin Timberlake at the 2001 American Music Awards

Ex. *'Was driving past Hillsong yesterday and spotted a gaggle of Coota Suits headin' inside to praise the Lord ...'*

Cul-De-Sacs

/ ˈkʌl-də-sæks /

1. A balding head that has crossed over from simply a receding hairline and is now beginning to resemble a suburban dead-end street
2. To exhibit male-pattern baldness at the very front of one's head, on either side of the fringe
3. Official hairstyle of the local cop

Ex. *'My hairline is weak as shit. Look at these Cul-De-Sacs ...'*

Dubbo Dinner Jacket

/ ˈdʌboʊ ˈdɪnə ˌdʒækət /

1. A flannelette shirt
2. A plaid or tartan shirt crafted with soft woven flannel fabric, often purchased from budget hometown outfitters
3. Comfortable overshirt appreciated by tradies and grunge rock enthusiasts

See also: Cobain Coat

Ex. *'When it's too hot for a hoodie but too cold for a polo, Glenn likes to slip on his favourite Dubbo Dinner Jacket ...'*

EB Games Moustache

/ i bi ˈɡeɪmz məˌstaʃ /

1. An underwhelming teenage moustache, located above the top lip of an adolescent male
2. Mandatory facial hair for EB Games staff and suburban Woolworths trolley pushers

See also: Bum Fluff

Ex. *'Me cousin Owen just turned 15, turned up to Nan's birthday rocking a new EB Games Moustache ...'*

Fitness Thirst Pants

/ ˌfɪtnəs ˈθɜst pænts /

1. Tight-fitting yoga pants worn by botoxed gym junkies to attract attention on their Instagram squat rack videos
2. A pair of leggings worn by F45 trainers in an attempt to increase membership sign-ups

Ex. *'Ethan's such a sleaze, his whole Instagram feed is girls doing TikToks in their Fitness Thirst Pants ...'*

Flog Clogs

/ ˈflɒg klɒgz /

1. Doc Martin shoes
2. A leather school shoe worn by private school hipsters with small feet
3. The official footwear of Brunswick, styled by music journalists and people who carry their wallet and phone in a New York Art Gallery gift shop tote

See also: Brunswick Creepers

Ex. *'Took me an age to get breakfast this morning, the cafe was heaving with the clip clop of all the Flog Clogs ...'*

Frenzal Ropes

/ ˌfrɛnzəl ˈroʊps /

1. Dreadlocks on a white person
2. Entangled locks of hair, matted or braided together, popular with West End and Northern Rivers hippies and individuals with dubious hygiene

See also: Trustafarian

Ex. *'Now that he's got a family, I think it's time we spoke to Adam about chopping off his rank Frenzal Ropes ...'*

Grain-Fed Mullet

/ ˈɡreɪn-fɛd ˌmʌlət /

1. An all-natural, pesticide-free, grain-fed Australian mullet, sighted in the regional country towns of Australia

Hairdresser notes: Military buzzed front and sides, extensive length flowing in the back, fully covering the neck

Notable figures: Jai Arrow; Bailey 'Bazlenka' Smith

See also: Nyngan Neck Warmer

Ex. *'Headin' up to Kurri Kurri this weekend for Mulletfest, gonna see some proper Grain-Fed Mullets in the wild …'*

Hungry Jackboots

/ ˌhʌŋɡri ˈdʒækbuts /

1. A pair of ugg boots
2. A unisex sheepskin boot, lined with fur or fleece, worn in cold climates for warmth and comfort
3. Nationally recognised footwear of the late-night Hungry Jacks pilgrimage

Note: Often spotted at Stockland shopping centres and early-morning netball matches

Ex. *'Vicky had a late-night craving for nuggets, so she slipped on her Hungry Jackboots, jumped in the Barina and ducked down to the fast food corner …'*

Jesus Jandals

/ ˈdʒizəz ˌsændls /

1. A Birkenstock sandal
2. Nationally recognised sandal of the coastal fuckboy
3. Official footwear of the pseudo-vegan farmers market micro-influencer, any bloke with a serious girlfriend

See also: Jerusalem Cruisers; Sawtell Sandals

Ex. *'I ran into Hamish in Harris Farm, he's a new man with the Jesus Jandals …'*

MJ Bail

/ ɛm dʒeɪ ˈbeɪl /

1. Cheap, highly flammable suit purchased from Tarocash or Politix
2. Machine washable, skinny fit pants, best styled with white loafers and Speed Dealer sunnies
3. Official criminal court attire of high-range drink drivers
4. Flemington or Doomben race day attire, optimised for Black Rat–fuelled trackside punch-ons

Ex. *'Tyson's court hearing is on the 15th, so me and Mum gotta take him down to the shops and get him fitted for a new MJ Bail ...'*

MAFS Mouth

/ ˈmæfs maʊθ /

1. A budget filler injection in the lips
2. Official facial filler of the *Married at First Sight* contestant
3. An injection of hyaluronic acid into the lips to 'improve' one's physical appearance

See also: Trout Pout; Kuta Kisser

Ex. *'You see that selfie of Sharnie from school? Looks like she went to Bali and came back with a MAFS Mouth ...'*

Mosman Gumboots

/ ˈmɒsmən ˌgʌmbuts /

1. R.M. Williams Craftsman boots
2. Official pavement-pounding footwear of the Concrete Cowboy, a city-dwelling finance professional who's never ridden a horse or lived on a farm

See also: Stockbroker Sneakers; Toorak Timberlands

Ex. *'There's nothing a Concrete Cowboy loves more than spending his bonus on a new pair of Mosman Gumboots ...'*

Pinger Polo

/ ˈpɪŋə ˌpoʊloʊ /

1. A party shirt worn by a hipster funboy
2. A bright, flamboyant shirt worn by speakeasy bartenders, music festival enthusiasts and Scomo on a Hawaiian holiday

Popular patterns: Watermelons, pineapples, vertical stripes (see also: Cotton On, Jay Jays)

See also: Bartender's Blouse

Ex. *'Before rolling into Groovin the Moo, James and the boys stopped by Jay Jays to pick up their Pinger Polos ...'*

Private School Pluggers

/ ˌpraɪvət skul ˈplʌɡəz /

1. A pair of Havaiana thongs
2. Overpriced footwear worn by yuppies on coastal holidays
3. A Brazilian brand of flip-flops charging upwards of $25 for two slabs of rubber

See also: Noosa Slippers

Ex. *'I busted a thong so I had to duck into the surf shop and blow $30 on a pair of Private School Pluggers ...'*

Puberty Perfume

/ ˈpjubəti ˌpɜfjum /

1. Lynx Africa body spray
2. An exotic mix of warm African spices and aromas worn by Australian teenagers

See also: Cineplex Spray

Ex. *'I was flying up to the Goldie and got stuck sitting next to some young fella who'd marinated himself in Puberty Perfume ...'*

Queen Street Mullet

/ ˈkwin strit ˌmʌlət /

1. A gentle, office-friendly variation of the Australian mullet, suitable for the workplace
2. A Monday–Friday watercooler mullet styled by city professionals

Hairdresser notes: Short choppy top, 0→2 faded sides with soft, curled length left in the back

Notable examples: The entire AFL; Nathan Cleary

See also: Mosman Mudflap

Ex. *'Gotta head down to the shearers for a back-to-work haircut, gonna ask the barber for a Queen Street Mullet ...'*

Recedes-Benz

/ rəˈseɪdiz bɛnz /

1. Early male pattern baldness
2. A follicly challenged male with a receding hairline and increasingly large forehead

See also: Cap Collector

Ex. *'Ever since Mark caught a case of the Recedes-Benz, poor bloke's been dropping cash on Mosh pills every week ...'*

School Shooter

/ skul ˈʃutə /

1. A trenchcoat
2. A full length men's coat, once made popular by Nick Cave, but nowadays more likely associated with American spree-shooters

See also: Peaky Blinder

Ex. *'No one could pull off a School Shooter like David Bowie ...'*

Speed Dealers

/ ˈspid ˌdiləz /

1. Sunglasses purchased from a service station
2. Wraparound-style sunglasses with reflective lenses, often lime-green or yellow

See also: Goog Goggles; Petrol Pump Pradas

Ex. *'Mate, I jagged myself a shiny new pair of Speed Dealers from the Shell this arvie …'*

Sticky Lid

/ ˈstɪki lɪdz /

1. A bucket hat
2. Wide-brimmed headwear worn by peacocking touch footy players, members of the rock band Sticky Fingers, Western Sydney drill rappers and primary school children

See also: Newtown Akubra; Halfback's Helmet

Ex. *'Gotta go to Cotton On and put my Splendour outfit together. Need to jag myself a few party shirts and a rainbow Sticky Lid …'*

Wanker's Waistcoat

/ ˈwæŋkəz ˌweɪstkoʊt /

1. A North Face puffer vest
2. An overpriced gilet worn by real estate agents, Super Rugby fans and F45 gym trainers
3. Official chestwear of the Hinge fuckboy

Note: Often styled with Mosman Gumboots, AirPods and a Queen Street Mullet

Ex. *'Went to an open house on Saturday and the AirPod with Legs was waltzing about in a Wanker's Waistcoat …'*

STYLE & FASHION

Weber Wheels

/ 'weɪbə wilz /

1. A pair of white New Balance sneakers
2. Leather cross-trainers loved by dads whose feet require wide fittings, i.e. 2E or 4E
3. Official shoe of the backyard BBQ grill master, lawn enthusiast and Indian grandmothers

See also: Grill Masters; Bunnings Brogues

Ex. *'Had no idea what to get Dad for his birthday, so I got him some Darrell Lea licorice and a fresh new pair of Weber Wheels ...'*

CHAPTER VI

Dining & Cuisine

Like our pandemics, public servants, celebrities, archetypes and clothes, we also give special names to the things we eat.

Many are just abbreviations and acronyms, but they don't really count and have been widely omitted from this chapter of Betoota-isms. The B&E roll, the BLT, the Spag Bol, the Large Cap with Two. Lazy nicknames that are so simple we forgot what they stand for.

That leaves only the true terms of reference that the people in Betoota use, inside our unspoiled monoculture of remote sameness.

Items such as the Bachelor's Handbag, for example. To the casual observer, it's just a roast chicken in a plastic bag from a supermarket. In our town, it's an accessory. A status symbol.

In fact, local by-laws stipulate that you must be a bachelor to buy a roast chicken from a supermarket. It's also illegal for a bachelor to drive into town without his mother's permission. But it's things like this which showcase what Betoota is about.

This chapter isn't about poking fun at the fact that this backwater colony only had two recipes before the ethnics arrived for the Snowy Mountains scheme. It's also not about poking fun at how prominent those two meals still are. *The Betoota Advocate* staff Christmas party has rotated between both of them over the last couple of years.

It's also not just about the many different migrant cuisines that Australia has controversially claimed as our own over the years. In the words of Darryl Kerrigan, 'But it's what you do with them, love!'

The two meals are silverside beef and lamb casserole, by the way.

365ers

/ θri sɪks ˈfaɪvəz /

1. Mutton chops, because farmers will eat them 365 days a year and never get sick of them
2. A small cut of sheep served with potato, two veggies and gravy (if you're lucky)

See also: Rawlinna Dinner

Ex. 'Brian never complains about walking into the kitchen and smelling a frypan sizzling with 365ers …'

Amex Breakfast

/ ˈæmɛks ˌbrɛkfəst /

1. A ham and cheese croissant and a soy latte, purchased for $16 at an airport lounge
2. Preferred breakfast of the Qantas lounge business professional, flying interstate for a one-hour meeting

Ex. 'Henry was flying Mosman to Melbourne for a client meeting, so he treated himself to an Amex Breakfast on the company card …'

Bachelor's Handbag

/ ˌbætʃələz ˈhændbæg /

1. A Woolworths roast chicken
2. Official lunch/dinner of the single male
3. A discounted multipurpose roast chook, which can be used to fill out toasties or 2 Minute Noodles

Note: Often purchased with a six-pack of white bread rolls, homebrand coleslaw and a longneck

Ex. 'Couldn't be arsed to cook last night, so I picked up a Bachelor's Handbag and some Maxibons on my way home from work …'

Bangkok Happy Meal

/ bæŋˈkɒk ˈhæpi mil /

1. Chicken pad thai and can of Diet Coke
2. $10 lunch special, purchased from the local Thai restaurant
3. A noted hangover cure

Alternative order: A pad see ew and can of Fanta

See also: Phuket Picnic

Ex. *'Mate, I'm absolutely starving, might go for a wander and buy myself a Bangkok Happy Meal …'*

Barina Brekky

/ bəˌrinə ˈbrɛki /

1. A McCafé iced coffee, a hash brown and a vape
2. Official drive-through breakfast of the regional bachelorette

See also: Boost Juice and a Digital Durry

Ex. *'Rebekah at Allure Hair & Beauty always walks in halfway through a Barina Brekky …'*

Black Doctor

/ blæk ˈdɒktə /

1. 375ml can of full strength, full sugar Coca-Cola
2. A scientifically proven cure for a hangover or food poisoning

Note: Not to be confused with a Skinny Bitch (Diet Coke)

Ex. *'Was feeling rotten with a bad case of the Grog Horrors, whipped through the servo and picked up a can of Black Doctor to set me straight …'*

Brickie's Brunch

/ ˌbrɪkiz ˈbrʌntʃ /

1. Cheese and bacon rolls (six-pack) and a 600ml red Gatorade
2. Convenient smoko/morning tea purchased at Bakers Delight

See also: Caltex Canapé

Ex. 'Started at 5 am today, so I swung past Bakers Delight and picked up a bit of Brickie's Brunch ...'

Caltex Canapé

/ ˌkæltɛks ˈkænəpeɪ /

1. Meat pie and 600ml chocolate milk/iced coffee, purchased from a service station as part of a meal deal combo
2. A convenient Caltex snack, a bundled deal of considerable value

Optional extra: Snickers or Crunchie bar

See also: Boilermaker's Breakfast; Gocsy Granola

Ex. 'Gotta get to the job site early tomorrow, will have to pick up a Caltex Canapé on the way ...'

Chinese Breath Mints

/ tʃaɪˈniz ˌbrɛθ mɪntz /

1. A packet of grey market cigarettes originally from China
2. Illegal imported cigarettes, purchased from a dodgy tobacconist

See also: Dongguan Darts

Ex. 'That corner shop up there sells Chinese Breath Mints for $10 ...'

Chozzie

/ ˈtʃɒzi /

1. A hybrid fusion of Australian and Chinese cuisine
2. A selection of mystery meats covered in unnaturally bright fluorescent sauces
3. A meal often served from the bain-marie of an RSL or bowling club buffet

Notable dishes: Mongolian Lamb; Honey King Prawn; Sweet 'n' Sour Pork; Special Fried Rice

Ex. *'Tuesday nights down at the bowlo ... they do a bloody good schooner and Chozzie buffet special ...'*

Concreter's Caviar

/ ˌkɒnkritəz ˈkævia /

1. A can of tuna
2. A tinned can of mystery aquatic animals brined in olive oil and various other flavours
3. Budget lunch consumed by protein-obsessed gym junkies, van-life hippies and office workers at the end of their pay cycle

See also: Last Dollar Lobster

Ex. *'Dragging my feet towards payday, going to have to suffer through a can of Concreter's Caviar for lunch ...'*

Darlo Breadline

/ ˈdaloʊ ˌbrɛdlaɪn /

1. An Instagram-famous bakery that requires an extensive wait in line
2. A local bakery charging upwards of $12 for a loaf of artisanal flour, yeast and water
3. Official Saturday-morning hobby of the PR marketer or craft brewer

Ex. *'Sorry mate, I'm stuck in a Darlo Breadline, I'll be a while ...'*

Moreton Bay Porridge

/ mɔtn ˌbeɪ ˈpɒrɪdʒ /

1. A cocktail of Bundaberg Rum and dairy milk.

Ingredients: 45ml Bundaberg UP Rum, 200ml icy-cold farm fresh milk, 3 ice cubes
Method: Combine ingredients in a cocktail shaker. Shake four times. Strain into a schooner glass filled with ice. Sometimes with a splash of vanilla essence.

Ex. *'Nothing warms up the heart in the morning like a glass of Moreton Bay Porridge and a dart when I'm out on the river ...'*

Paddington Tankwater

/ ˌpædɪŋtən ˈtæŋkwɔtə /

1. San Pellegrino sparkling mineral water
2. A luxurious Italian water stored in a glass bottle, used to impress rich neighbours or business clients at a long lunch
3. Water enjoyed by Range Rover drivers and yuppies who spend every June in Europe

Ex. *'Hughie's new misso is a bit bougie, she won't drink from the tap, only ever orders that Paddington Tankwater ...'*

Pavement Sprayer

/ ˈpeɪvmənt ˌspreɪə /

1. A late-night kebab
2. A flatbread stuffed with doner meat shavings, salad and a glorious mixture of herb and garlic sauces, consumed outside of a nightclub after a big night out

See also: Sidewalk Pizza

Ex. *'After Jake and I got kicked out of the Caxton, we went and got ourselves a Pavement Sprayer and caught an Uber home ...'*

Plumber's Picnic

/ ˌplʌməz ˈpɪknɪk /

1. A KFC Zinger Box and a Solo/Sunkist
2. Official lunch of the plumber, concreter or labourer

Optional extras: Popcorn Chicken and a Twix

See also: Fried Bird Box

Ex. *'Mitch couldn't be assed putting a sambo together, so he treated himself to a Plumber's Picnic for lunch …'*

Rat's Coffin

/ ˈrætz ˌkɒfən /

1. A sausage roll
2. A grey mystery meat entombed in a tube of burnt flaky pastry, served with sauce at sporting events, service stations and school canteens

See also: Pork Twinkie; Cessnock Cannelloni

Ex. *'Running late to the job site, so whipped into the servo and picked up a Rat's Coffin and a Strawberry Oak …'*

Rolling Sizzler

/ ˌroʊlɪŋ ˈsɪzlə /

1. Yum cha
2. An all-you-can-eat dining experience where a selection of dim sum, dumplings and noodles is served from a trolley pushed by an elderly Chinese waiter

Ex. *'Gotta take Mum out for her birthday, thinking we might go treat her to brunch at the Rolling Sizzler …'*

DINING & CUISINE

Soggy Blocks

/ ˈsɒgi blɒks /

1. A bowl of Weet-Bix
2. Rectangles of wholegrain wheat flakes, drenched in milk and topped with fruit, honey or sugar
3. An Australian breakfast eaten by kids before sporting matches

Ex. *'Had crook guts all week, so I've been chewing through nothing but bowls of Soggy Blocks …'*

Sponsored Continental

/ ˈspɒnsəd kɒntəˌnentl /

1. An açaí bowl
2. A breakfast bowl made from blended açaí berries, topped with fruits, nuts and various hyped foods
3. Preferred breakfast of Instagram influencers and people who have to take a photo of everything they eat

Ex. *'After her barre class, Becky likes to go down to Bondi and 'gram a bowl of her Sponsored Continental …'*

Tuesday Frisbee

/ ˌtjuzdeɪ ˈfrɪzbi /

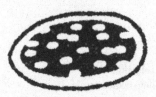

1. A cheap Tuesday pizza
2. A $5 pizza of limited nutritional value, consumed by university students and Riverina Rollie enthusiasts
3. The lucrative reselling of slices considered a popular fundraising initiative implemented at high school out-of-uniform days

Notable flavours: Margarita; Meatlovers; Hawaiian; 4-Ingredient 'Supreme'

Ex. *'I found $10 in my wallet so I decided to treat myself to a Tuesday Frisbee and a lava cake …'*

CHAPTER VII

Liquor & Gaming

The two great Australian pastimes: doing your arse on the punt, then doing your arse on the grog. If you do both things things regularly, you should stop and seek help.

When you really get in the hammock and think about it, these two things are responsible for so much anguish in this country. Can you imagine being a recovering gambling addict in Australia? You can't watch a fucking game of sport without having odds rammed down your throat by some bloke who's one strained vowel away from blowing his voicebox out like Darren Lockyer.

On top of that, imagine trying to get off the piss. You've got ad after ad on the television telling you that you can't even hang out with your mates without getting blackout drunk on mid-strength beer. Can't go fishing, can't go to the cricket. Can't grill meat without getting some fucking piss inside you.

What do I know? I'm only a newspaper journalist who indulges in both of these vices with wanton abandon. There's nothing that predatory advertising agencies can tempt me with that wasn't already forced onto me by the busted reporters I was assigned to as a 16-year-old cadet.

Either way – problematic or not – the pub bistro, the pub gaming lounge and the pub itself play a major part in the fabric of Australian society. And it's not going away anytime soon. The only hurdle this cultural institution has ever faced was the introduction of the random roadside breathalyser.

However, not all of the terms of reference in this chapter exclusively ascribe to alcohol and gambling. As a 47-year-old confirmed bachelor, I am also partial to the extracurriculars that come with courting fast women and betting on slow horses.

If you don't know what I'm implying with that comment, then it might be worth skipping over the next few pages and googling the nearest aeroplane hangar so you can spend your weekends clapping to deodorised Christian rock like our wowser Prime Minister does. But be wary – a lifestyle centred around buying forgiveness from a man with bleached teeth probably does cost more.

A Raging Bull

/ ˈreɪdʒɪŋ bʊl /

1. A Red Bull mixed with 45ml of Bundy Rum
2. A potent mix of taurine, pyridoxine HCL and North Queensland Fighting Fluid

See also: Gordon's Gunpowder

Ex. *'I was fallin' asleep in the beer garden so I ordered two Raging Bulls and bloody oath it got me fired up …'*

Bert Newton

/ bɜt ˈnjutn /

1. To lose one leg on a multi
2. A long-legged multi (an Ostrich) that fails due to one unfortunate misplaced wager

Notable culprit: A concussed Anytime Tryscorer

See also: A Bee's Dick

Ex. *'I was so close to banking $500 off a fiver but the Thai women's ping-pong leg blew out and I ended up with a Bert Newton …'*

Black Rat

/ ˈblæk ræts /

1. A 375ml can of Bundy 'n' Coke
2. Official canned spirit of B & S balls and regional Rugby Union team bus trips
3. A potent mix of North Queensland Fighting Fluid and Black Doctor

See also: Sin Tins; Can of Fight

Ex. *'Over the weekend I went down to the Deni ute muster and ripped through a brick of Black Rats …'*

Blue Rocket

/ blu ˈrɒkət /

1. Balter XPA
2. Tropical and fruity Extra Pale Ale, brewed in Currumbin, Queensland

Awards: #1 GABS Hottest 100 XPA (2018)

See also: Can of Fanno

Ex. 'Mate, come round on Saturday, getting the crew together for a BBQ and some Blue Rockets in the sun ...'

Booze Buffet

/ ˈbuz ˌbʌfət /

1. An open bar tab or function drinks package funded by a workplace or father-in-law
2. Office work party function to celebrate Silly Season and Christmas festivities

Notable beverages: Peroni/Crown Lager; cleanskin red or white wine; Brain Varnish

See also: Schooner Smörgåsbord; An Open Zoo

Ex. 'I've got a head like a bag of nails, went too hard on the Booze Buffet at our work Christmas party last night ...'

Brain Varnish

/ ˈbreɪn ˌvanɪʃ /

1. A cheap spirit priced under $10 a bottle
2. Noxious grog that quickly erodes brain cells; can also be used as weed killer or pest control

Notable examples: Cleanskin schnapps; black market Ukrainian vodka

Ex. 'Heard Graham is a massive booze hound who'll drink anything, even that Brain Varnish ...'

Brickie's Laptop

/ ˌbrɪkiz ˈlæptɒp /

1. Pokie machine
2. Digital gambling computer found in VIP lounges of pubs, clubs or RSL establishments

Notable machines: Lucky 88; Queen of the Nile; More Chilli; Where's The Gold?

See also: Plumber's PlayStation; Mount Isa MacBook

Ex. *'Rain closed down the job site, so me and the boys gonna go do some bookwork on the Brickie's Laptop ...'*

Cardboardéaux

/ kadbɔdˈdoʊ /

1. Cask red wine
2. A boxed wine that can be mixed with homebrand orange juice to make 'sangria' at university house parties

See also: Bathurst Briefcase

Ex. *'I gotta go down to Woolies, pick up a fresh box of Jatz to pair with that red Cardboardéux ...'*

Caxton Street Car Bomb

/ ˈkækstən strit ˌka bɒm /

1. A schooner of XXXX Gold Lager mixed with a 45ml shot of Bundy Rum
2. The official Caxton Street cocktail
3. A delicious concoction of Queensland mid-strength lager and Sugarcane Champagne

See also: Brisbane Bellini

Ex. *'Needed to fire up before the big game so I knocked back two Caxton Street Car Bombs at the Paddo Tav ...'*

Christian Cocaine

/ ˈkrɪstʃən koʊˌkeɪn /

1. An espresso martini
2. A potent coffee-flavoured cocktail made with vodka, coffee liqueur, espresso and sugar syrup
3. A legal substance that is the closest thing you can consume to cocaine

Ex. *'After polishing off two rounds of Christian Cocaine, Tahlia and her squad hit the dancefloor ...'*

Coward's Cordial

/ ˌkaʊədz ˈkɔdiəl /

1. A hard seltzer
2. A low-carb alcoholic mineral water, a naturally fermented beverage enjoyed in summer by individuals frightened by calories

Ex. *'Chloe's on a health kick, so she's been sipping on that Coward's Cordial every time we go out ...'*

Crims on Rims

/ ˈkrɪmz ɒn ˈrɪmz /

1. Harness racing, 'the trots'
2. Sport in which standardbreds are harnessed to a two-wheeled cart (a sulky) and raced around a trotting track

See also: Roman Raceway; Corruption Chariots

Ex. *'My uncle knows the barman at Albion Park, he passed on a sure thing for the Corruption Chariots this weekend ...'*

Digital Durry

/ ˈdɪdʒətəl ˌdʌri /

1. An e-cigarette
2. Any variety of vape, vape pen or electronic device used to smoke tobacco

See also: WiFi Winnie Blue; Panasonic Puff Stick

Ex. *'I'm tryna quit smokin' darts and eat more fruit, so I'm into them grape and mango Digital Durries …'*

Dishlickers

/ ˈdɪʃlɪkəz /

1. Greyhound racing
2. A sport in which greyhounds are bred and raced for the sole purpose of problem gambling

See also: Dapto Dogs

Ex. *'My wife's brother is one of those sickos who actually has tips for the Dishlickers …'*

Double Parked

/ ˌdʌbəl ˈpakt /

1. To be in possession of two alcoholic beverages at the same time
2. To stockpile drinks on a night out, a technique used among intellectuals to limit the short walk to the bar

Ex. *'Oi keep an eye on your nephew, he's been double parked for most of the night. We all know how this ends …'*

Fax Machine

/ ˈfæks mə ˌʃin /

1. To use an in-venue TAB machine to place a bet
2. Preferred method of betting for the over-60s punters, and NRL players who are banned from having apps on their phones

See also: To Bet Race 8 on the Windows 98

Ex. *'I dropped my phone in the urinal so I had to log my multi on the Fax Machine …'*

Gatorade Saxophone

/ ˈgeɪtəreɪd ˌsæksəfoʊn /

1. A homemade bong
2. A apparatus used to smoke marijuana, usually constructed with a garden hose and an empty Gatorade bottle

Ex. *'Nathan spends his lunch break ripping solos on his Gatorade Saxophone down the back of the IGA carpark …'*

Grog Horrors

/ ˈgrɒg ˌhɒrəz /

1. To be suffering from the anxious effects of excessive drinking and hedonistic extracurricular activity
2. The niggling feeling deep within that you have said or done something that will come back to haunt you while on the piss
3. Also known as 'The Fear' in Ireland

See also: PPA (Post-Piss Anxiety)

Ex. *'Jesse won't pop up till Monday I don't think, she's got a real bad case of the Grog Horrors …'*

Hermit Park Handshake

/ ˈhɜmət pak ˌhænʃeɪk /

1. To punch a pub patron in the face, named after the light industrial Townsville suburb of Hermit Park, home to some of North Queensland's most hot-headed railway workers.
2. To be hit with a closed fist during an altercation

Ex. *'It was a rowdy night down at O'Malley's, saw a few Hermit Park Handshakes …'*

Hinch's Hermès

/ ˈhɪntʃəs hɜˌmez /

1. A cask of crisp white wine
2. A five-litre box of Coolabah Sweet Fruity or Fresh Dry White
3. Affordable boxed wine hung from clotheslines at regional university parties
4. The chosen drink of proper drinkers, such as former Federal Senator Derryn Hinch

See also: Frankston Fruit Bag

Ex. *'Turned up to the cousin's baby shower and Aunt Kylie was pissed as a parrot after finishing off a cube of Hinch's Hermès …'*

Kaftan Diesel

/ ˌkæftæn ˈdizəl /

1. Sparkling white wine
2. A cheap prosecco served in bulk at open bar functions and office Christmas parties

See also: Woo Girl Fuel

Ex. *'For Mel's 50th, the girls went out for a bottomless brunch and got stuck into the Kaftan Diesel …'*

Mackay Yoga

/ məˌkeɪ ˈjoʊɡə /

1. A police operation which results in a line-up of individuals on their knees, with hands cuffed behind their backs
2. A significant criminal bust concerning the importation of illicit substances/firearms/illegal wildlife trade, or any police activity that results in mass arrests

See also: Port Botany Pilates

Ex. *'I was driving past Macca's and saw about five cop cars with lights flashing, teaching a bit of Mackay Yoga to those Cowboys fans that were starting fights ...'*

Milton Mango

/ ˌmɪltn ˈmæŋɡoʊ /

1. XXXX (pronounced 'Four Ex') Gold
2. Iconic Queensland mid-strength lager, brewed in Milton, Brisbane

See also: Lockyer Lager

Ex. *'Wally and Alan are coming round to watch the footy this arvie, we'll be good for a few Milton Mangos in the sun if you're keen ...'*

Nose Beers

/ ˈnoʊz bɪəz /

1. Cocaine
2. An illegal substance derived from the leaves of the coca plant, manufactured into a white powder [$C_{17}H_{21}NO_4$] and snorted via the nasal cavity

See also: Bondi Marching Powder; Prahan Pixie Dust

Ex. *'Did ya hear Jackson got kicked out of the pub after getting caught snortin' Nose Beers off the pub porcelain ...'*

Old Mate Out Front

/ oʊld ˈmeɪt aʊt frʌnt /

1. A delivery of cocaine
2. A bag drop, often received over the tinted window of a Subaru WRX STI

See also: Your mate, our mate, Thingo

Ex. *'Mate, can you hurry up and find an ATM – I'm waiting for a text from Old Mate Out Front …'*

Put on a Spider

/ pʊt ɒn ə ˈspaɪdə /

1. To put on an eight-leg multibet
2. To put together an outrageously long multi with multiple variants of winning teams, Anytime Tryscorers and odd foreign sports

See also: Green Caterpillar

Ex. *'Mate, I've put on a ripper spider, just need Vadim Putilovsky to win the Ukrainian table tennis and I'll make an easy grand …'*

Riverina Rollie

/ rɪvəˌrinə ˈroʊli /

1. Cannabis, marijuana
2. The dried leaves and flowers of the cannabis plant, smoked for recreation
3. The third biggest export from the New South Wales Riverina behind wine and Murray Darling water licenses

See also: Devil's Lettuce; Vegan Cigarette; Mullumbimby Marlboro

Ex. *'Our youngest Kaylah is a bit of a free spirit, she's spent the last decade in Byron Bay, playing bongos on the beach and smoking a bit of Riverina Rollie I think …'*

Russian Handball

/ ˌrʌʃən ˈhændbɔl /

1. Obscure betting markets used to thicken up a multi bet with various additional legs including, but not limited to, Korean ping-pong, Serbian ice hockey or Canadian curling
2. To gamble on foreign sports with no reasonable knowledge or understanding

Ex. *'Jimmy is a mug punter, do not listen to him. He's always fattening up his multi with Russian Handball …'*

Schooey Schooey Moi Moi

/ ˈʃui ˈʃui ˈmɔɪ mɔɪ /

1. A freshly poured beer enjoyed while watching Rugby League football
2. Official beer of the NRL forward

See also: Ale Finucans; Tin Glasbys; Jahrome Brews

Ex. *'We drinking pints or the Schooey Schooey Moi Mois?'*

Speaking Greek

/ ˌspikɪŋ ˈgrik /

1. To be heavily intoxicated
2. To have temporary mental and physical impairment due to the effects of alcohol or recreational substances

Symptoms: Slurred speech, incoherent rambling, lack of coordination, inability to make smart decisions

See also: Hammered; Tanked; Blind

Ex. *'Last night the hubby and I ripped through a Square Bear, and by god we were Speaking Greek …'*

Stonefruit Smoothie

/ ˌstoʊnfrut ˈsmuði /

1. Stone & Wood Pacific Ale
2. Hazy Australian Pale Ale with fresh tropical fruit flavours and aromas

See also: Byron Bay in a Bottle; Fruit Salad Saison

Ex. *'My sister is coming around with her new man for dinner. He works in media so I've had to stock up on the Stonefruit Smoothies …'*

Sugarcane Champagne

/ ˌʃʊɡəkeɪn ʃæmˈpeɪn /

1. Bundaberg Rum/Bundy Rum
2. Biblical holy water produced and enjoyed in South East Queensland
3. Official fighting fluid of North Queensland

See also: Cane Cutter's Cordial; Square Bear; Biff Syrup

Ex. *'You've always gotta be careful on a night out in North Queensland, those pubs are full of blokes who fill up on the Sugarcane Champagne and throw hands …'*

Todd Carney Cottees

/ tɒd ˈkɑni ˌkɒtiz /

1. Vodka Cruiser
2. A potent, brightly coloured pre-mixed vodka
3. Beverage enjoyed by schoolies, Canberra Raiders footballers and Suzuki Swift drivers

See also: Goulburn Gatorade

Ex. *'Had a shit of a day, so me and Blake went and drank a six-pack of Todd Carney Cottees on the roof …'*

Townsville Sunrise

/ ˌtaʊnzvɪl ˈsʌnraɪz /

1. A glass of fresh pineapple juice mixed with 45ml of Bundy Rum and a dash of lime
2. A North Queensland breakfast cocktail

See also: Mackay Mimosa

Ex. *'Before a big day on the combine harvester, Gordon starts his morning with a fresh Townsville Sunrise ...'*

Truckie's Toothpaste

/ ˌtrʌkiz ˈtuθpeɪst /

1. Illegal amphetamines
2. An illegal synthetic stimulant, known to increase energy, alertness and agitation

See also: Goey; The Whizz Fizz

Ex. *'Ya hear Boof got the boot from the job site? He tested positive to having a bunch of Truckie's Toothpaste in his system ...'*

VCR

/ vi si ˈa /

1. A vodka, Coke and raspberry cocktail
2. A popular alcoholic beverage in Newcastle, NSW.

See also: The Blood of the Steelworks

Ex. *'After the Knights pumped Manly, Joey ordered a round of VCRs for the boys down at the Queen's Wharf Hotel ...'*

Victor Bravo

/ ˌvɪktə braˈvoʊ /

1. Victoria Bitter, stubbie or tin
2. The aviation codewords for a thirst-quenching full-strength VB

See also: Victoria Beckham; Green Demons; Hand Grenades

Ex. 'Mate, I'm just whipping into town to pick up a case of Victor Bravos for the footy this weekend ...'

White Eggs

/ ˈwaɪt ɛgz /

1. A 375ml can of Jim Beam Bourbon & Cola
2. Official refreshment of the Mount Panorama petrolhead or local big shot at a country pub
3. A sweet, fizzy and gritty alcoholic beverage

See also: Summernats Spritz

Ex. 'Me and Clint are heading up the mountain tonight to bury a nest of White Eggs for Bathurst next weekend ...'

Sports

Sports

It's a cliché to say sport is at the centre of our national identity. We like it, sure, but it's not all that there is to us.

Politicians and their friends in the media will have you believe it is, but that's only because they are overeducated and out-of-touch. Desperate to find something to dangle in front of us that makes us smile.

They were too busy last century scratching each other's backs and trying to impress the Queen to notice that everyone had stopped going to church every Sunday morning, and when that finally became clear, they started showing up at our footy ovals on Sunday afternoons.

It was around the same time that Catholics were finally considered whitefellas that John Howard pulled together the spectacular Sydney 2000 games. Since then, we've been told that all we fucking care about is sport.

A key example of this is the fact that nobody wanted the 2020/21 Tokyo Olympics to go ahead. When you think about it, sending our young people over to Japan to take part in such an event at a time like this is borderline criminal. Government policy around the so-called developed world dictates that nobody should be travelling. You should not go overseas if you don't absolutely have to. But it was better for our government to be talking about how few gold medals we'd won than it was to be talking about how few vaccines they'd ordered.

But in saying all of that self-righteous shit above, I don't think anybody is too upset at the prospect of having even more sport to watch.

At the time of writing, our cricketers are over in the West Indies getting absolutely thrashed in a bit of hit and giggle. They got there on a privately chartered Qantas 787 Dreamliner which flew directly from Brisbane to the Caribbean. Sure, a few people were upset at the unnecessary travel, but I don't think people are losing sleep over it.

Cricket is our national sport. Every state plays it.

The winter is split geographically. Wagga Wagga is the line. Rugby League up north. Victorian Rules down south.

There're also a few other sports, like Rugby Union. Rugby Union is played all over the world and was quite popular in Australia before its administrative bodies became stacked with the same useless political class mentioned above. They'll be back, though. We just need to wait it out until the dead wood rots.

Nearly every town in Australia has a golf club and Australians are typically pretty good at golf. It's the only sport where you're allowed to talk about how good you are. That's because the 'handicap' – a universal numerical measurement of a golfer's potential – provides us with a humble guise to hide behind while we brag.

To be truly great at sport in this country, to be a sporting legend, you need to deny your talents to the point where even you're surprised that you're now a world champion.

Let everyone else talk about how good you are.

1st Gen Footy

/ fɜst ˈdʒɛn ˈfʊti /

1. Soccer, European football
2. A sport played with a round ball, popular among first-generation Australians
3. Internationally regarded as the 'The World Game', fourth most popular ball-based sport in Australia

See also: Divegrass; Foot Marbles

Ex. *'Been trying to sign Luca up to play touch footy with us but he loves his 1st Gen Footy …'*

American Netball

/ əˈmɛrɪkən ˌnɛtbɔl /

1. Basketball
2. A sport played on a court where two teams of five players attempt to toss an orange ball into a hoop to score points
3. Particularly popular with abnormally tall Australians and people who indulge in expensive sneakers

Ex. *'Andrew is close to seven feet tall, no wonder he's so good at American Netball …'*

Big Hooah

/ bɪg ˈhua /

1. A stocky rugby playing male, built to play prop forward
2. A big rig with plump calves and a meaty neck of considerable girth

Enjoys: Ruckin 'n' maulin'; hit-ups; bringing it home in the final leg of a post-match boat race

Notable Big Hooahs: Shane Webcke, Matt Dunning, George Rose

Ex. *'Went down to watch the 4ths play … Christ there were some Big Hooahs getting around this year …'*

Bogan Silks

/ ˌboʊgən ˈsɪlks /

1. A modern polyblend football jersey
2. Rugby League sportswear made with a high percentage of synthetics and flammable polyesters, as opposed to the traditional saggy cottons

See also: League Lycra

Ex. *'I was up in Brisbane for Magic round and the entire city was bursting with fans in their Bogan Silks ...'*

Cattledog

/ ˈkætldɒg /

1. A call to arms to start an on-field fistfight during a match of Rugby League
2. An on-field physical altercation resulting in the exchange of fists
3. To honour the great Tommy Raudonikis (OAM) by starting a chop

See also: The Biff; A Stink; A Scrap; A Blue; A Barney

Ex. *'Nothing frightens a Queenslander more than the Cattledog ...'*

Four-Legged Lottery

/ fɔ-ˈlɛgəd ˈlɒtəri /

1. Horse racing
2. A sport in which two or more thoroughbred horses are raced for the purpose of sport, entertainment and gambling
3. A multimillion-dollar industry filled with corruption, animal cruelty and race fixing

Origins: A famous novel by Frank J Hardy

Ex. *'Put on some good clobber, we are heading to Flemington for the Four-Legged Lottery tomorrow ...'*

SPORTS

Functional Alcoholism

/ ˈfʌŋkʃənəl ˈælkəhɒlɪzəm /

1. Golf
2. An expensive club and ball sport, where players attempt to hit a small white ball into a shallow hole in the ground
3. A leisurely tempo sport enjoyed by retirees, businessmen and Donald Trump

Ex. *'Jason and his mates went on a bucks' trip, swear they spent the whole weekend playing 18 holes of Functional Alcoholism …'*

Keyhole Ball

/ ˈkihoʊl bɔl /

1. Netball
2. A sport played by two teams of seven, aiming to shoot a ball into a raised hoop
3. A recreation which always results in keyhole surgery, funding physiotherapists' ski trips

Ex. *'Poor Kerry's on light duties cos she's done her knee playing Keyhole Ball again. This is her sixth ACL, there's no tendons left!'*

The Milk

/ ðə mɪlk /

1. Canberra Raiders Rugby League team
2. Established in 1981, a team that came to prominence with the CANBERRA MILK sponsor in the centre of their jersey

Notable players: Josh 'Big Papi' Papalii, Hudson 'The Branxton Bulldog' Young

See also: The Green Machine; Mal's Milkmen

Ex. *'Keen to see the Panffers take on Canberra tonight, I reckon The Milk might actually get the win …'*

Mungo

/ ˈmʌŋɡoʊ /

1. Rugby League
2. A popular variant of rugby football, where two sides of 13 players bash, batter and run over the opposition in the attempt to score a try with a Steeden branded football
3. A rough sport popular on the east coast of Australia, predominately in Western Sydney and South East Queensland

Ex. 'Heading down to Orange to watch the City vs Country, looking forward to watching some world-class Mungo ...'

The National Sport

/ ðə ˈnæʃnəl spɔt /

1. Cricket
2. A sport played with a bat and ball, where two teams of 11 players attempt to score runs by jogging between wooden stumps at either end of a pitch
3. The barometer of our country's success and national morale

Also known as: The Great Distraction, as no matter what's happening in the news cycle, it can always be trumped by a story about a reshuffle of the Aussie batting order

Ex. 'Heading to Melbourne for Boxing Day, I've got tickets to watch The National Sport from Bay 13 at the MCG ...'

SPORTS

Nut Trucker

/ 'nʌt 'trʌkə /

1. Straight and hard runner of the Rugby League football
2. NRL forward able to transport the ball from A to B without footwork, flair or finesse
3. A term coined by the *Hello Sport* podcast, of number one Australian sporting podcast fame

Key traits: City vs country representative duties; lacks ball-playing skills or the ability to offload the football

Notable alumni: Danny Nutley (GOAT), Nigel Plum, Shane Tronc, Martin Lang

Ex. *'Great to see a few specialist Nut Truckers hooking in this season, bit too much kicking last year ...'*

Rah Rah

/ 'ra ra /

1. Rugby Union
2. A less popular variant of rugby football, where 15 sides attempt to score points with a Gilbert football
3. A brand of football played by private schools and country towns in the New England electorate

Ex. *'Going to my workmate's bucks party in Sydney to watch the Tahs vs the Reds in the Rah Rah ... Something different ...'*

Rough Riding

/ 'rʌf ˌraɪdɪŋ /

1. Bull riding
2. A rodeo event where a bull rider attempts to stay on top of a bucking bull for up to eight seconds
3. A sport popular in the rural heartlands of Australia, the American south and Brazil

Ex. *'We're off to the Mount Isa Rodeo this weekend to witness some world-class Rough Riding ...'*

Rural Networking

/ ˈrurəl ˌnɛtwɜkɪŋ /

1. Polo
2. A sport played on horseback, where two teams of four players use a long mallet to score a goal
3. A snobby equestrian sport played by Blue Bloods and the wealthy rural elite

Ex. *'Kathy from Armidale jumped in her Prado and drove up to Scone for the Rural Networking this weekend ...'*

Victorian Leg Tennis

/ vɪkˌtɔriən ˈlɛg ˌtɛnəs /

1. Australian Rules Football or AFL
2. Leather ball sport enjoyed by the southern states of Australia, Western Australia and the Northern Territory
3. A sport disregarded by New South Wales and Queensland residents

See also: St Kilda Ballet; Brunswick Badminton

Ex. *'I'm heading down to Memorial Park to watch the Deni Rovers play a bit of Victorian Leg Tennis ...'*

Water Torture

/ ˈwɔtə ˌtɔtʃə /

1. Swimming
2. A sport where individuals race by propelling themselves through water
3. A sport in which young people are forced to stare at a straight black line for the duration of their formative years
4. An Olympic event recognised as initiating Australia's trade war with China

Ex. *'Always thought James was a bit of a weirdo, apparently he went to the Youth Olympics for Water Torture, so that probably explains it ...'*

Sports Stars

They say the highest office in the country is not that of Prime Minister, it is Captain of the Australian Test Cricket Team.

Anyone can be the Prime Minister; you just have to be a ruthless sociopath that looks like a breakfast sausage in a suit. You need to be a pathological liar and be okay with being loathed by half the country and barely tolerated by the other half.

Not much is really expected of them.

Our sport stars are required to be perfect, otherwise lesser media outlets like to cut them down. They're human, these highly strung athletes who have spent a decade getting ready to play sport at such an elite level. Of course they're going to make mistakes.

And if the kid making those mistakes doesn't look like a Hemsworth, you better believe the back-page outrage merchants will whip them all the harder.

In America, shock jocks use words like 'thug' to denigrate black athletes who offend the white upper middle-class sensibilities of the establishment. In Australia they say 'sook'.

White kids get it too, but not as bad, unless they have scary tattoos or an unconventional haircut.

However, the tide is slowly turning in the world of media pile-ons. The players now have bigger followings of adoring fans on social media than any Murdoch hack has readers.

The power imbalance has faltered. These days it's nothing for a 23-year-old to tell some drunken Baby Boomer at Fox Sports to suck his dick on Twitter and get applauded for doing it.

We at *The Betoota Advocate* say good luck to them. The real villains here are the pearl-clutchers acting like they can't see how fun it is to wear a nun's outfit and drink 20 beers on Mad Monday while furiously messaging Instagram models.

It is also said that you're not truly a sports star in this country until you receive your own unique nickname from the wider Australian public. Some nicknames come from the press and those ones are usually terrible and should be omitted.

Think of all the greats – they've all had their own.

The Accountant

/ ðə əˈkaʊntənt /

1. Cameron Smith
2. Former Melbourne Storm, Queensland Maroons and Australian Rugby League hooker; future Immortal

Career highlights: Two Golden Boot Awards (2007, 2017); the NRL's most capped player of all time (430 games); highest ever NRL pointscorer (2786 points)

Famous for: A haircut you could set your watch to; looking more like an accountant than one of the greatest ever to play the game

Ex. *'You gotta wonder whether The Accountant would pull an MJ and make a comeback for the right price ...'*

The Albury All-Star

/ ðə ˈælbəri ˈɔl-sta /

1. Lauren Jackson
2. Celebrated Australian basketballer for the Australian Opals and Seattle Storm

Career highlights: Three-time WNBA MVP (2003, 2007, 2010); Australian Olympian; inducted into the Naismith Memorial Basketball Hall of Fame (2021)

Famous for: Being Australia's most decorated basketballer; being from Albury

Ex. *'Was playing a game of mixed down at the Lauren Jackson Sports Centre and I had to mark up against The Albury All-Star herself...'*

Alexander the Great

/ æləgˈzændə ðə greɪt /

1. Alexander Volkanovski
2. Featherweight UFC champion of Macedonian descent, like Alexander the Great
3. Former prop for the Warilla Gorillas

Famous for: Being the Fighting Pride of Shellharbour

Ex. 'I saw Alexander the Great helping his old man old pour some concrete in the Gong last weekend. He's still a good Illawarra boy at heart ...'

Bala Pat

/ ˌbɔlə ˈpæt /

1. Patty Mills
2. Indigenous basketballer for the San Antonio Spurs and the Aussie Boomers. His nickname 'Bala' is derived from the Torres Strait Islander creole term for 'brother'

Career highlights: Winning an NBA championship with the San Antonio Spurs (2014); three-time Olympian representing Australia

Famous for: Launching Indigenous Basketball Australia (IBA) to empower Indigenous Australian athletes

Ex. 'Jeez, it's good to see Bala Pat back in the green and gold ... He's always good for a buzzer beater.'

Bam Bam

/ bæm bæm /

1. Tai Tuivasa
2. Heavyweight UFC fighter; mixed martial artist proudly representing Western Sydney

Famous for: Introducing 'the shoey' to the UFC; dishing out hidings on the world stage

Ex. 'Anyone got a stream for the main event? I wanna watch Bam Bam put on another beat-down ...'

Barty Party

/ ˈbati ˈpati /

1. Ash Barty
2. World No 1 Australian tennis player; former cricketer; unanimously liked by the entire country
3. National Indigenous Tennis Ambassador for Tennis Australia

Famous for: Being the pride of Ipswich; restoring the nation's faith in tennis

Ex. *'I was at the Hotel Metropole and you wouldn't believe who won the members' raffle, it was Barty Party, taking home the meat tray in straight sets …'*

Big Tuna

/ bɪg ˈtjunə /

1. Kyle Chalmers
2. Australian freestyle swimmer, six-time Olympic medallist

Career Highlights: Silver medallist at the 2020/21 Tokyo Olympics in the 100m freestyle; gold medallist at the 2016 Rio Olympic Games

Ex. *'You seen the shoulders on the Big Tuna? No wonder he can swim faster than a Yellowfin …'*

Binga

/ ˈbɪŋə /

1. Brett Lee
2. Former Australian fast bowler
3. Decorated right-arm pace bowler with 76 Test matches and 310 Test wickets for Australia
4. Bollywood star, highly regarded for his Oscar-nominated performance in *unIndian* (2015)

Famous for: Being an early pioneer of blond frosted tips; having a nickname honouring the Bing Lee chain of electrical stores

Ex. *'Imagine facing an over of hot-tempered seamers from Binga, that would've been a nightmare back in the day …'*

Bruce's Wet Dream

/ ˈbrusɪz wɛt ˈdrim /

1. Winx
2. Retired champion racehorse

Career highlights: Considered the greatest racehorse of all time, with 33 consecutive race wins including 25 group wins

Famous for: Bringing racing commentator Bruce McAvaney to climax multiple times

Ex. *'Sure there were Phar Lap and Black Caviar, but none of them come close to the records broken by Bruce's Wet Dream ...'*

Dizzy

/ ˈdɪzi /

1. Jason Gillespie
2. Former Australian right-arm fast bowler

Career highlights: 259 wickets in 71 test matches for Australia

Famous for: Championing the nineties pirate aesthetic; a nickname honouring the American jazz trumpeter Dizzy Gillespie

Ex. *'I miss the days of the two-headed pace attack of Pigeon and Dizzy ...'*

The Eighth

/ ðə eɪtθ /

1. Andrew 'Joey' Johns
2. The Eighth Rugby League Immortal, highly regarded as the greatest Rugby League footballer of the modern era
3. Former halfback for the Cessnock Goannas, Newcastle Knights, State of Origin Blues and Australian Kangaroos

Famous for: Two Newcastle Knights premierships (1997, 2001); inventing the banana kick; falling asleep at the Toowoomba Airport in 2015

Ex. *'Did ya hear there's a petition going round to get a gold statue of The Eighth out the front of Newcastle Stadium ...'*

The Floating GOAT

/ ðə ˌfloʊtɪŋ ˈɡoʊt/

1. Emma McKeon
2. Australian Olympic swimmer, considered Australia's greatest ever Olympian

Career highlights: Hauling in a total of 11 Olympic medals (5 gold, 2 silver and 4 bronze) between the 2016 Rio and 2020/21 Tokyo Games

Ex. *'Heard Qantas had to schedule in another cargo plane to bring home all the silverware The Floating GOAT brought home …'*

The Flying Doormat

/ ðə ˈflaɪŋ ˌdɔmæt /

1. Bruce Doull
2. Former Carlton Football Club defender

Career highlights: Four Carlton premierships (1972, 1979, 1981, 1982)

Famous for: An unrivalled mop of hair and mutton chops

Ex. *'If you wanna talk about wild footy haircuts, nothing comes close to the luscious locks of The Flying Doormat …'*

Funky

/ ˈfʌŋki /

1. Colin Miller
2. Former Australian fast-medium bowler

Career highlights: 69 wickets in 18 Tests for Australia

Famous for: A colourful history of hairstyles

Ex. *'Not many could swing it around the pitch as well as Funky …'*

Garrrrrry

/ ˈgɛərrrrrri /

1. Nathan Lyon
2. Australian off spinner

Career highlights: 399 wickets in 100 Test matches for Australia

Famous for: Ascending from a career as the pitch caretaker at the Adelaide oval to an all-time Australian Test cricketer; having the same last name as an AFL great

Ex. 'Noice one, Garrrry ...'

God

/ gɒd /

1. Gary Ablett Snr
2. Former Hawthorn and Geelong Australian Rules footballer

Career highlight: Three-times Coleman Medal winner and inductee in the Australian Football Hall of Fame

Famous for: Supreme goal-kicking ability; blaming the Covid-19 pandemic on the Illuminati and Freemasons' desire to create a new world order

Ex. 'A Geelong legend, I tell ya there's never been a greater kicker of the Sherrin than God ...'

Helmet

/ ˈhɛlmət /

1. Tim Horan
2. Former centre for the Queensland Reds and Australian Wallabies

Famous for: A perfectly sculpted head of hair; being able to commentate Rugby Union without sounding patronising

Ex. 'I don't know what hair gel Helmet uses, but that stuff is tough as concrete ...'

Honey Badger

/ ˈhʌni ˌbædʒə /

1. Nick Cummins
2. Former winger for the Western Force and Australian Wallabies
3. Reality television star who appeared on *The Bachelor* (2018)

Famous for: His tucker bag packed to the brim with Australian vernacular; baggin' plenty of meat (scoring lots of tries) for the Force; giving himself a nickname; deciding to not enter into an arranged marriage on live television

Ex. *'Honey Badger had a good game last night, he was going off like a cut snake …'*

Jingles

/ ˈdʒɪŋgəlz /

1. Joe Ingles
2. Basketballer for the Utah Jazz and the Aussie Boomers

Career highlights: Holds the Utah Jazz franchise record for most three-pointers

Famous for: Bringing a taste of Aussie banter to the NBA; causing James Harden headaches

Ex. *'Switch over to the NBA, I wanna watch Jingles pot some threes for the Jazz …'*

Kalyn the Alien

/ ˈkeɪlɪn ðə ˈeɪliən /

1. Kalyn Ponga
2. NRL fullback for the Newcastle Knights and Queensland Maroons

Famous for: Being the second hottest Newcastle Knight after Connor Watson; his schoolboy highlights; being interested in art and shit

Ex. *'Heading out to the Kingdom to watch the Knights this arvo, I've heard Kalyn the Alien is fit and ready to rip …'*

The King of the North

/ ðə ˈkɪŋ əv ðə ˈnɔθ /

1. Johnathan Thurston
2. Champion Indigenous All Star, three-times Golden Boot winner (2011, 2013, 2015)
3. Former halfback for St Mary's College, North Queensland Cowboys, Queensland Maroons and Australian Kangaroos

Famous for: The eight-in-a-row Queensland State of Origin streak; having the greatest laugh in Rugba Leeg; delivering Townsville their first ever NRL premiership (2015)

Ex. *'I was wandering down along the Strand and I swear I heard the King of The North's laughter echoing out of the Seaview Hotel ...'*

Korea

/ kəˈriə /

1. Dean Waugh
2. First-class cricketer, the often-forgotten Waugh

Ex. *'Sure there was Mark and Steve, but no one ever remembers Korea ...'*

Kyng Kyrgios

/ ˈkɪŋ ˈkɪriɒs /

1. Nick Kyrgios
2. Australian professional tennis player
3. Brat born in Canberra; athletically gifted player with an extensive history of on-court misconduct

Famous for: Volatility; shouldering the hopes of Australia during the January spike of interest in tennis

Ex. *'Did ya see Kyng Kyrgios is back in the winner's circle at Roland-Garros ...'*

Ley Ley

/ ˈleɪ leɪ /

1. Lleyton Hewitt
2. Former World No 1 Australian tennis champion; Order of Australia medallist
3. Adelaide Crows' number one ticketholder

Career highlights: Two-time Grand Slam singles champion (US Open 2001, Wimbledon 2002); 2001 ATP Player of the Year

Famous for: Marrying *Home and Away* actor Bec Cartwright; his signature court cry of 'C'mon!!'

Ex. *'Ley Ley and Beck are our Royal Family.'*

Madame Butterfly

/ ˌmædəm ˈbʌtəflaɪ /

1. Susie O'Neill
2. Celebrated Australian swimmer, inducted into the Sport Australia Hall of Fame (2002)

Career highlights: Winner of eight Olympic medals; gold medal at the 2000 Sydney Olympics in the 200m freestyle

Famous for: An illustrious career winning medals in butterfly and freestyle

Ex. *'Do you remember where you were the day Madame Butterfly won that gold at the Sydney Olympics ...'*

Family Court

/ ˌfæmli ˈkɔt /

1. Margaret Court
2. Former World No 1 women's tennis player

Career highlights: 24 x Grand Slam singles championships; Australia's most decorated tennis player

Famous for: Boycotting Qantas over its support of same-sex marriage; having a stadium named after her, which may no longer be the case by the time this book is published

Ex. *'Read in the news old lady Family Court's been at it again, calling us all heathens for letting the gays get married …'*

Mr TikTok

/ ˌmɪstə ˈtɪktɒk /

1. David Warner
2. Top order Australian batsman; former captain of the national team

Famous for: Unleashing an unexpected TikTok career during the Covid-19 pandemic

Ex. *'Nothing brings the SCG to their feet like a fired-up Mr TikTok slogging it to the boundary …'*

Nobody

/ ˈnoʊbɒdi /

1. John Eales
2. Former Australian Wallabies captain; inducted into the Sport Australia Hall of Fame (2003)
3. A kicking second-rower

Famous for: The golden era of Australian Rugby Union; being nicknamed for the expression 'nobody's perfect'

Ex. *'Work put on a corporate lunch last week and Nobody came to give a bit of a speech about resilience.'*

The One Eyed Blue

/ ðə ˈwʌn-aɪd blu /

1. Phil 'Gus' Gould
2. Australian Rugby League broadcaster, player, administrator and coach

Career highlights: All-time most successful NSW Blues coach; appointed Member of the Order of Australia

Famous for: Origin pre-game rev-up speeches; stealing Laurie Daley's chair on the sidelines at the 2003 State of Origin; being slightly biased towards NSW

Ex. *'Had to watch the Channel Nine footy broadcast last night and my god! It was tough listening to all of the absolute dribble coming out of The One Eyed Blue …'*

Pez

/ pɛz /

1. Ellyse Perry
2. Australian women's all-rounder, the youngest Australian to ever play international cricket

Career highlights: Represented Australia at World Cups in two different sports (soccer and cricket)

Famous for: An illustrious career across multiple sports

Ex. *'Spotted Pez down at the nets doing another three-hour session with the English Willow …'*

Pigeon

/ ˈpɪdʒən /

1. Glenn McGrath
2. Former Australian fast-medium pace bowler

Career highlights: 563 wickets in 124 test matches for Australia, one of two fast bowlers to have entered the '500' club

Famous for: Lanky legs; learning to bowl by pacing balls at a 44-gallon drum in Narromine, NSW

Ex. *'Wanna talk about consistency, Pigeon had a line and length you could set your watch to …'*

Punter

/ ˈpʌntə /

1. Ricky Ponting
2. Former captain of the Australian cricket team; top order batsman

Career highlights: Four-times Allan Border Medalist, second most runs in International Test Match history (13,378)

Famous for: Being nicknamed after his early career fondness for punting on the Dishlickers

Ex. *'Punter did a lot for cricket, but I reckon his biggest contribution was that PlayStation 2 game …'*

The Queen

/ ðə kwin /

1. Yvonne Sampson
2. NRL sports presenter and commentator
3. Universally loved TV anchor, the host of Fox Sports' *League Life*

Famous for: Being nicknamed the Queen of Rugby League

Ex. *'Oi, would yas shut up! I can't hear The Queen give her post-game analysis …'*

The Raging Bull

/ ðə ˈreɪdʒɪŋ bʊl /

1. Gorden Tallis
2. Queensland Maroons legend, considered one of the best second-row forwards of all time

Career highlights: Three-times Grand Final winner with the Brisbane Broncos (1997, 1998, 2000); winner of the 1998 Clive Churchill Medal

Famous for: Raw, unbridled on-field aggression; rag-dolling Blues fullback Brett Hodgson over the sideline in Game III of the 2002 State of Origin

Ex. *'Spotted The Raging Bull dragging his suitcase off the bag carousel at Brisbane airport. I tell ya what, he's still got it …'*

Rocket Rod

/ ˈrɒkət rɒd /

1. Rod Laver
2. Australian Tennis Champion, nine-times World No 1

Career highlights: 11 Grand Slam singles championships

Famous for: Having that arena named after him where the Foo Fighters and Ed Sheeran always play

Ex. *'Did you know the greatest ever to play tennis, Rocket Rod, was born in Rockhampton …'*

Skull

/ skʌl /

1. Kerry O'Keeffe
2. Former Australian spin bowler and cricket commentator

Famous for: Spinning good yarns during tea break

Ex. *'The Skull has a laugh like a '93 Commodore that needs a new exhaust …'*

Sharon Woods

/ ʃəˌrɒn ˈwʊdz /

1. Aaron Woods
2. NRL prop forward for the Wests Tigers, Bulldogs, Sharks, NSW Blues and Kangaroos

Famous for: Luscious locks of hair; having one of the most uncreative nicknames in Rugby League

Ex. *'Good to see Sharon Woods finally get stuck in and have a crack tonight …'*

Skippy

/ ˈskɪpi /

1. Geoff Huegill
2. Former Australian butterfly swimmer

Famous for: Being an Olympic silver and bronze medallist; an Oprah-esque fluctuating waistline

Ex. *'Was doing laps down at the Betoota Aquatic Centre and I was sharing a lane with Skippy, he's trimming down again ...'*

Son of God

/ sɒŋ əv ˈgɒd /

1. Gary Ablett Jnr
2. Descendent of Gary 'God' Ablett Snr; Geelong and Gold Coast midfielder often considered one of the greatest AFL players of the modern era

Career highlights: Two-times Geelong premiership winner (2007, 2009); dual Brownlow Medallist (2009, 2013)

Famous for: Continuing the famous Ablett name in the sport of AFL

Ex. *'Was watching the Cats last night and that Son of God sure takes after his father in the kicking department ...'*

Spag Bol

/ ˈspæg boʊl /

1. Peter Bol
2. Australian middle-distance runner born in Khartoum, Sudan

Career highlights: Representing Australia at the 2020/21 Tokyo Olympics and placing fourth in the 800m final

Famous for: Discovering he was pretty quick after running at a school athletics carnival

Ex. *'I spotted Spag Bol running a few laps of the city last night. I couldn't keep up, he was beating me to every set of lights ...'*

The Taree Ferrari

/ ðə taˈri fəˈrari /

1. Latrell Mitchell
2. South Sydney Rabbitohs fullback
3. Talented Rugby League footballer from the New South Wales mid north coast

Famous for: Taree Red Rover Junior; Indigenous All Star; NSW Blues; two-times Premierships with the Sydney Roosters (2018, 2019)

Ex. *'Mate, I'm keen as to watch The Taree Farrari rip through his old mates at the Roosters tonight. Glory Glory ...'*

The Terminator

/ ðə ˈtɜməneɪtə /

1. Ariarne Titmus
2. Australian Olympic swimmer from Launceston, Tasmania

Career highlights: Gold medal winner in the 400m and 200m freestyle at the 2020/21 Tokyo Olympics

Famous for: Having half the country screaming at the TV whilst stuck in lockdown

Ex. *'I heard The Terminator likes doing laps across the Bass Strait! Only takes her a few hours to swim from St Kilda to Devonport ...'*

Test Match

/ ˌtɛst mætʃ /

1. Mario Fenech
2. South Sydney Rabbitohs club legend who played every match as though it was a test match

Career highlights: Captained the 1998 Prime Minister's XIII

Also known as: The Maltese Falcon

Ex. *'I miss the days of seeing old Test Match on the telly for the Thursday night footy show ...'*

Thorpedo

/ θɔˈpidoʊ /

1. Ian Thorpe
2. Decorated Australian swimmer

Career highlights: Five-time Olympic gold medallist; Young Australian of the Year (2000)

Famous for: Having size 17 feet and swimming like a fuckin' torpedo

Ex. *'Sure miss those 2000 Olympics when the Thorpedo was smashing world records like guitars …'*

The Throat

/ ðə θroʊt /

1. Darren Lockyer
2. Former NRL five-eighth and fullback; Brisbane Broncos and Queensland Maroons legend

Career highlights: Two-times Golden Boot Award winner (2003, 2006); highest ever capped Brisbane Broncos player (355 games)

Famous for: Having a throat as coarse as the Gabba pitch on day 3

Ex. *'Don't mind a bit of panel commentary from The Throat, he always cuts through the bullshit …'*

Tommy Turbo

/ ˌtɒmi ˈtɜboʊ /

1. Tom Trbojevic
2. NRL fullback for the Manly Sea Eagles and NSW Blues
3. Brother to Jake Trbojevic; collectively known as the nicest brothers in Rugby League

Famous for: Impressive speed and ability to score millions of tries for the Peninsula; racing drunk Manly punters down the Manly Corso

Ex. *'I was down in Manly and saw Tommy Turbo helping an old lady cross the road …'*

Tongan Thor

/ ˈtɒŋən θɔ /

1. Taniela Tupou
2. Tight head prop for the Queensland Reds and Australian Wallabies

Famous for: Being a 132kg prop with the passing skills of a flyhalf; a YouTube video from his high school days playing in New Zealand that got him signed to the Super Rugby

Ex. *'God forbid the day I have to tackle the Tongan Thor ...'*

The Toowoomba Pumba

/ ðə təˌwʊmbə ˈpʊmbə /

1. Matty Denny
2. Australian discus thrower from Allora, QLD

Career highlights: Representing Australia at the 2016 Rio and 2020/21 Tokyo Olympics

Famous for: Throwin' a dinner plate further than ya nan can walk; being a big strong farm fella

Ex. *'Did ya see The Toowoomba Pumba throwin' last night? Will be givin' 'im a call next time I gotta load the ute ...'*

Victor the Inflictor

/ ˈvɪktə ðə ɪnˈflɪktə /

1. Victor Radley
2. NRL middle forward for the Sydney Roosters and NSW Blues
3. Former Clovelly Crocs junior

Famous for: Being one of the NRL's favourite naughty boys; severing a man's head with his shoulders

Ex. *'Spotted Victor the Inflictor making the most of his week off, he was putting back a few schooners at the Cloey Hotel ...'*

The Voice

/ ðə vɔɪs /

1. Ray 'Rabbits' Warren
2. The Voice of Rugby League; legendary NRL sports commentator honoured with an Order of Australia medal

Famous for: Providing the 'soundtrack of winter' for over four decades

Ex. *'It's just not Rugba Leeg unless the TV is blaring with the heavenly tones of The Voice ...'*

Waltzing Matt Hilder

/ ˌwɔlsɪŋ mæt ˈhɪldə /

1. Matt Hilder
2. Former NRL utility for the Cronulla-Sutherland Sharks, Gold Coast Titans and Newcastle Knights

Ex. *'One of the best NRL super-subs was Waltzing Matt Hilder, put him anywhere and he'd plug the hole ...'*

The Wizard

/ ðə ˈwɪzəd /

1. Simon Whitlock
2. Australian professional darts player

Career highlight: Winner of the 2012 European Championship

Famous for: An exceptional beard and dreaded-pony-tail-mullet

Ex. *'Nath goes alright at the darts, he could almost take on The Wizard for a title ...'*

CHAPTER IX

Town & Country

There is a small divide between the city and the bush, but this chapter isn't necessarily about that. Even though the Fortunate Sons who end up in the LNP try to make out that people in the city don't understand what it's like for regional Australia, they don't do a very good job of addressing what life is like for some poor prick on a crowded train heading off to an inner-city rat's nest to run on a fucking giant hamster wheel for some tax-dodging corporation that could replace them with someone else in less than a day.

Anyway, this chapter aims to break down this divisive rhetoric, and highlight the parallels you'll find between the metropolitan suburbs and regional communities like Betoota.

There are common threads that weave our towns and cities together. Certain shops and places of that ilk are found in every part of the country. Also in this chapter, we look at the shared aspirations of kids in the bush and the big smoke. Places like the National Institute of Dramatic Art (NIDA) are defined by how we view them in our town. People in Betoota often refer to NIDA as 'Clown School' because to a regional Queenslander, there's little value in amateur and professional theatre. It's a cultural appendix, they say. There are two amateur theatre companies in Betoota, and they hate each other.

Another thing that's common across every Australian town is having a local shire council that is corrupt to the core. In fact, if a council isn't corrupt then it's probably not doing its job, which is to rort and extort money from state and federal governments, pay themselves handsomely, then build a second skatepark for a town of 700. But only if there's some-one on the council who owns a concreting business. People in Betoota refer to our council chambers as 'The Trough'. Not because every councillor in town looks like a bi-pedal pig, but because they all get their fill before they let anybody else in.

The Queensland Crime and Corruption Commission (CCC) has been out to Betoota countless times but they've never been able to make anything stick. Our Mayor Keith Carton (Teflon Keith) is bloody bad and good at it. Unstoppable. In fact, at this rate, the only way Keith can be stopped is by a disenfranchised young man looking out the seventh-storey window of the Betoota Heights Schoolbook Depository with an Italian-made centrefire rifle in his hands.

Well, that's probably enough to get you started on this chapter.

Aviary

/ ˈeɪvjəri /

1. The airport
2. A fleet of commercial aeroplanes, likely grounded due to the pandemic

Ex. *'Drove past the Aviary yesterday, could hear all the Jetstar planes rusting away …'*

The Big Blue Bin

/ ðə bɪg blu ˈbɪn /

1. The ocean
2. The large expanse of sea water that surrounds Australia, often disrespected by waterfront workers who can't be fucked walking 20 metres to a garbage bin

Ex. *'You should've seen the wharfies throwing their durries and offcuts into The Big Blue Bin. They need to watch some Attenborough …'*

Canberra Conveyor Belt

/ ˌkænbrə kənˈveɪə bɛlt /

1. Elite private schools, known for producing 'the leaders of tomorrow'
2. Pretentious colleges of education and privilege

Key characteristics: Straw boater hats; half-hearted Rugby Union fandom; nepotism

Notable locations: North shore of Sydney; inner-east Melbourne; NSW Southern Highlands

Ex. *'You can tell that Connor has come straight off the Canberra Conveyor Belt, he just told me that the government should slash funding for women's shelters …'*

Cancer Shop

/ ˈkænsə ʃɒp /

1. A dodgy tobacconist
2. A cigarette store that sells a variety of vapes, smoking paraphernalia and assorted NRL memorabilia

See also: that weird front counter at Woolies

Ex. *'I was stinging for a Mango vape so I went looking for a Cancer Shop ...'*

Cattle Tick

/ ˈkætl tɪk /

1. A Catholic
2. The predominantly white middle-class Australians who are riddled with guilt by a religion they may have lost touch with long ago

Ex. *'Jeez, that Barnaby Joyce doesn't really behave like a Cattle Tick, does he ...'*

Chippy's Pantry

/ ˌtʃɪpiz ˈpæntri /

1. A drive-through bottle shop
2. Convenient liquor store where alcohol and smokes can be purchased from the comfort of one's vehicle

See also: Schooner Servo

Ex. *'After a long week on the tools, Brian made a pit stop through the Chippy's Pantry ...'*

Clog Wog

/ ˈklɒg wɒg /

1. A person of Dutch or Scandinavian background

Ex. *'We've got Isaak playing striker this week, crafty with the boot. Always good to have a Clog Wog up front ...'*

Clown School

/ ˈklaʊn skul /

1. NIDA
2. The National Institute of Dramatic Arts
3. Highly esteemed acting school that every single male Australian actor pretends they only went to because they lost a bet with their mates on a worksite

Notable alumni: Cate Blanchett; Mel Gibson; Baz Luhrmann

Ex. *'Spotted Hugo waiting tables down at the cafe, I think he's been struggling to find a job since graduating from Clown School ...'*

Curtain Shop

/ ˈkɜtn ʃɒp /

1. The Big 'n' Tall store
2. Gentlemen's outfitter that specialises in 3XL–7XL menswear
3. A fashion boutique for tight head props and Double Meatlover with Stuffed Cheesy Crust-type operators

See also: Sasquatch Store

Ex. *'George is a monster of a fella, poor bloke has to do all his wardrobe shopping at the Curtain Shop ...'*

Dead Centre of Town

/ ˈdɛd ˌsɛntə əv ˌtaʊn /

1. The local cemetery
2. Burial ground where townsfolk are laid to rest

Ex. *'Every time we drive to church, Grandpa always gives a nod to his mates in the Dead Centre of Town ...'*

Grandma's Carpark

/ ˌgrænmaz ˈkapak /

1. The auto-wreckers; car scrapyard
2. Burial ground of damaged vehicles, often the final resting place for spare parts and scrap metal

See also: Corolla Cemetery

Ex. *'Had a bad prang in the Volvo, had to call the tow truck and get it donated to Grandma's Carpark ...'*

Gravy Day

/ ˈgreɪvi deɪ /

1. National day of celebration for gravy, observed on 21 December
2. To honour Paul Kelly and the acclaimed Australian Christmas carol 'How to Make Gravy' (1996)

Notable characters in attendance: Dan; Joe; Stella; Angus; Mary; Frank and Dolly; Roger; Rita; Tomato Sauce

Ex. *'I'm stuck in lockdown and can't see the family. Paul Kelly sure tugs at the heartstrings this Gravy Day ...'*

Greek Broom

/ ˈgrik brum /

1. The garden hose
2. The Southern European practice of hosing down a driveway or heavily concreted courtyard for recreation, regardless of water restrictions

Ex. *'Is Spiro still on the driveway with the Greek Broom? He's been out there for hours ...'*

The Greeks

/ ðə griks /

1. Local independent supermarket that doubles as a cafe or milk bar
2. A large store that sells fresh produce, meat, bakery and dairy products

See also: The Corner

Ex. *'I've gotta head down to The Greeks this afternoon to pick up some tinned tomatoes for the bol …'*

The Long Drop

/ ðə ˈlɒŋ drɒp /

1. A caravan park
2. The area where retirees park their M1 Mansions and set up camp for a holiday

Ex. *'Doug and Hazel booked themselves in for a four-night stay at the Long Drop in Forster …'*

Her Majesty's Hotel

/ hɜ ˈmædʒəstiz hoʊˌtel /

1. Prison
2. A place of stay for criminals and those awaiting trial, funded (often poorly) by the Commonwealth

See also: The Holiday Inn

Ex. *'After getting involved in an ATM ram raid, Jimmy booked himself a nine-month stay at Her Majesty's Hotel …'*

Higher-Vis Education

/ haɪə-ˈviz ɛdʒəˈkeɪʃən /

1. TAFE
2. Vocational education and training provider, offering practical and industry-relevant courses
3. Skills factory supplying qualifications ranging from certificates to diplomas

Ex. *'Been telling my son not to waste his money on a degree, the kid should go get a trade at the Higher-Vis Education centre ...'*

Highway Hilton

/ ˌhaɪweɪ ˈhɪltn /

1. A three-star motor inn
2. A family owned and operated motel, offering affordable accommodation (including breakfast)
3. Roadside hotel located within 200 metres of a service station

Notable inclusions: 24 hour check-in; Austar; Continental breakfast; roof mirrors

Ex. *'I was roadtrippin' up to Hervey Bay, had a very pleasant one-night stay at the Highway Hilton in Coffs Harbour ...'*

Knock Shop

/ ˈnɒk ʃɒp /

1. The brothel
2. A business located in the red-light district where people engage the services of sex workers

See also: The pollywaffle

Ex. *'After a three-week swing in the FIFO camp, Justin visited just about every Knock Shop in Airlie ...'*

The Last Good Catholics

/ ðə ˌlast gʊd ˈkæθlɪks /

1. Filipino-Australians
2. Australia's most devout observers of Roman Catholicism, often employed in caregiver roles and cruise ship karaoke bands

Ex. *'I don't have to worry about a babysitter, mate, my wife's family are some of the Last Good Catholics …'*

The Last Resort

/ ðə ˌlast rəˈzɔt /

1. The casino
2. An entertainment venue filled with problem gamblers and vapid nightclubs
3. The last place open on a night out, destined to result in sadness

Ex. *'After getting kicked out of three pubs, Kyle and his mates had to settle for The Last Resort …'*

Leftie Factory

/ ˈlɛfti ˌfæktri /

1. A sandstone university
2. A pretentious tertiary education institution built pre-1900
3. A uni campus known for overpriced degrees and a flawed business model that relies on wealthy foreign students

Ex. *'Ran into Hugh the other day wearing a Young Greens shirt, not really a surprise after five years at the Leftie Factory …'*

The Mensa Club

/ ðə ˈmɛnsə klʌb /

1. The TAB
2. An in-venue gambling facility filled with unsung suburban geniuses

See also: The Screens

Ex. *'On Saturdays my Pop likes to head down to The Mensa Club and have bit of a flutter …'*

The Old Pom

/ ðə ˈoʊld pɒm /

1. A bulk-billing GP
2. Friendly senior local doctor with an English accent, the only bulk-billing general practitioner in town

See also: The Ten Pound GP

Ex. *'Feelin' like I might pull a sickie this week, gonna go visit The Old Pom and get a doctor's certificate …'*

Pensioner's Playground

/ ˌpɛnʃənəz ˈpleɪgraʊnd /

1. The bowling club
2. A recreational venue offering a variety of activities for elderly Australians

Ex. *'Maureen and Doreen spend most of their Thursdays down at the Pensioner's Playground for raffle night …'*

Pub with No Beer

/ ˈpʌb wɪð noʊ ˌbɪə /

1. A church
2. Place of Christian worship
3. The Sunday gathering place for Happy Clappers, Tupperware Christians and Devil Dodgers

Ex. 'My Gran is a devout Methodist, she spends a lot of time at the Pub with No Beer …'

Rissole

/ ˈrɪsoʊl /

1. Returned and Services League Club
2. An RSL club with licensed bar and dining facilities

Known for: Meat tray raffles; exotic carpets; Brickie's Laptops; moderately priced Australian-Chinese (Chozzie) buffet meals

See also: The Arey

Ex. 'Mate, come down to the Rissole on Thursday, they're doing a 2-for-1 Rump and Karaoke Night …'

Rumour Mill

/ ˈrumə mɪl /

1. A small-town hairdressing studio or beauty salon
2. Local source of all town gossip
3. Workplace of self-appointed local news correspondents specialising in scandalous rumour and speculation

See also: The Goss Shop

Ex. 'Did ya hear Brett's been shagging Kayla? The missus went to the Rumour Mill for a haircut and came back with all the gossip …'

School Zone

/ ˈskul zoʊn /

1. The suburb surrounding the local police station
2. A street where every driver travels under 40km/h to alleviate the anxiety of being caught speeding

Ex. *'Gotta go to the School Zone to report that bastard who stole my hubcaps last night ...'*

Schooner Shop

/ ˈskunə ʃɒp /

1. The pub
2. A licensed establishment where alcoholic beverages are sold and consumed
3. A local watering hole with freshly poured tapped beer and a TAB

Most popular names: The Royal; The Railway; The Imperial; The Commercial; The Courthouse

Ex. *'After a blister of a week, I'm meeting the boys down at the Schooner Shop where we are going to watch 160 minutes of high octane Rugby League on a 70 inch television ...'*

Sunburnt Sudoku

/ ˌsʌnbɜnt səˈdoʊku /

1. The boat ramp
2. A slipway located on a lake or harbour where boat owners attempt to loudly navigate a vessel into the water
3. A needlessly complicated stretch of concrete surrounded by great minds

Ex. *'Shane broke his ankle down at the lake, he slipped over while trying to drag the dinghy out of the Sunburnt Sudoku ...'*

The Trough

/ ðə trɒf /

1. The council chambers
2. The municipal council building which houses the local government authority
3. Responsible for the management of local recreational facilities, waste and sewerage, and the facilitation of small-town corruption

See also: The Swamp

Ex. *'I'm having a bust-up with council about that dodgy development, gotta make a visit to The Trough and sort those corrupt bastards out …'*

The Viets

/ ðə viˈɛts /

1. A French-style Vietnamese bakery often located in working-class suburbs and industrial estates
2. Bakehouse that offers a vast selection of bánh mì rolls, meat pies, a small variety of cakes, slices and tarts and an extensive range of soft drinks
3. Preferred lunch destination of the first year apprentice, university Arts student and travelling salesman

Ex. *'The boys were starving for smoko, so we trotted down to The Viets and picked up a Bung Knee and a can of Black Doctor …'*

The Wall of Knowledge

/ ðə ˈwɔl əv ˈnɒlɪdʒ /

1. The park bench at the footy oval
2. The place where former greats sit and shout unsolicited advice to the local sportsmen and women

See also: The Bench of Bullshit

Ex. *'Ian likes to spend his Sundays sitting at The Wall of Knowledge and reliving his sporting days …'*

White White

/ waɪt waɪt /

1. Protestants
2. Adherents of the Anglican Church
3. A brand of Christianity commonly associated with elitist attitudes due to the church's ties to the British monarchy, and Australia's history of oppressing every other religion but theirs

Ex. *'Mate, those White White families on the river still reckon Catholics shouldn't be allowed to vote ...'*

The Zoo

/ ðə zu /

1. The footy oval
2. The local sportsground where contact sports are played
3. A discreet local venue where Mad Monday celebrations are hosted away from the predatory cameras of local media.

Ex. *'Come down to The Zoo on Saturday arvo, the third grade boys are playing their Grand Final ...'*

CHAPTER X

Automotive

If you've never owned a car that was truly a piece of shit, just go ahead and rip this chapter out of the book and throw it in the bin. Because you'll never understand the unconditional love that Australians show towards an unreliable steel steed.

I'm not talking about those cars that are ten or fifteen years old that have an intermittent engine light. One that you take to a mechanic every six months and get charged half of what it would gain you to sell the fucking thing. The half-decent car you persist with even though the mechanic says you should just trade it in or simply commit some low-level insurance fraud and torch the cunt in a quiet street near the airport.

I'm talking about the cars that have a soul and that soul hates you. Like when you get in the fucking thing after a late shift; it's 2:37am and it's raining. You turn the key and the fucking starter just clicks at you like a cicada. Then you give it another go and it just gives you more lip. You punch the steering wheel and scream so loud that you hurt your throat. 27km from home and flat broke. Still sticky from working the main bar all night on your own. You could walk but you're no Jane Saville, you've just worked for 17 hours straight on your Nan's birthday and you're rooted. Not to mention rego is due in a month and now you've got a fucked car in some fucked part of town and you live on the other side. Plus you've just put a new tyre on it and dropped in a new battery.

These are the cars that these terms of reference relate to. These cars, and the cars we spent those late nights fantasising about. The cars that seem too good to be true.

I mean, imagine having enough coin to buy a Ford Ranger outright. Some people don't have to imagine, but those people are less likely to truly appreciate what they have.

Again, if you've only ever owned a nice car that hasn't fucked your life up at the worst possible time, then skip this chapter.

The Australian Dream

/ ðə əsˌtreɪljən ˈdrim /

1. A Ford Raptor
2. A 2.0-litre, twin-turbo diesel dual cab ute with double-wishbone front suspension, 238mm of ground clearance and custom leather trim
3. Official vehicle of the cashed-up FIFO coal mining professional

See also: Pilbara Porsche; Moranbah Mercedes

Ex. *'Me mate Kane just finished a six-week stint up at Newman, came back and blew all his money on The Australian Dream ...'*

Banglops

/ ˈbæŋlɒps /

1. Dodgy tyres
2. A cheap set of tyres, purchased in an effort to save money
3. 4 x stock tyres destined to burst after six months

See also: Shityears

Ex. *'Bit short of cash for my car rego, so I asked the spannerman to fit my Falcon with a cheap set of Banglops ...'*

Byron Bulldozer

/ ˈbaɪrən ˈbʊldoʊzə /

1. A Range Rover Sport
2. A black luxury SUV obnoxiously driven by yuppies and wealthy seachangers, as they participate in the great northern migration to Wategos Beach, Byron Bay
3. A poorly driven suburban utility vehicle, often spotted double-parked in an inner-city loading zone

See also: The Paddington Pickup; The Toorak Tractor

Ex. *'Took me an hour to get a park down at Belongil cos the whole place was swarming with Byron Bulldozers ...'*

Craptiva

/ ˈkræpɪvə /

1. A Holden Captiva
2. A budget mid-sized SUV, purchased by young parents unsure of how many kids they are going to have
3. Highly valued vehicle of the Saturday soccer/netball mum

Ex. *'Wendy took the Craptiva down to the auto boys for a service, it'd been making weird noises all week …'*

Dunny Door

/ ˈdʌni dɔ /

1. A Holden Commodore
2. An iconic medium to large sedan, manufactured in Australia from 1978–2020
3. Quintessential vehicle baked into Aussie automotive folklore

Ex. *'There's a bloke on Gumtree selling a 2005 VZ Dunny Door for $5000, gonna give him a ring and see if he'll knock the price down a bit …'*

Foot Falcon

/ ˈfʊt ˌfælkən /

1. Walking
2. The act of travelling by foot due to lack of access to a vehicle

See also: A Saunter

Ex. *'Had no luck hailing a taxi, so Ben and I had to Foot Falcon it home …'*

AUTOMOTIVE

Guangzhou Go-Kart

/ ˈgwʌŋ ˈdʒoʊ ˈgoʊ-kat /

1. A Great Wall Steed
2. A cheap 4X2 diesel single cab ute, manufactured in China, awarded an ANCAP 2-star safety rating (2016)

See also: A wish.com HiLux

Ex. *'My boss is such a tightarse, even our work fleet is a bunch of Guangzhou Go-Karts ...'*

High Horse

/ ˈhaɪ hɔs /

1. A Tesla
2. An overpriced luxury electric vehicle with less power than a AA battery
3. Preferred vehicle of tech start-up wankers and Melbourne Demons fans

Ex. *'George had to cut his Yarra Valley roadtrip short after his High Horse ran out of battery ...'*

Hot Laps

/ ˈhɒt læps /

1. To drive a vehicle up and down the main street of town in the company of mates
2. Driving for no real purpose or intent, purely 'checkin' out what's goin' on ...'

See also: Mainies

Ex. *'Oi brah, what ya doing? Riley got his Ps, we're gonna go do some hot laps and probably end up at Macca's ...'*

Landscaper's Lambo

/ ˌlændskeɪpz ˈlæmbaʊ /

1. A 2008 HSV Maloo Ute
2. Internationally recognised vehicle of the Monster Energy–drinking motocross enthusiast

Key identifiers: 19-inch black BBS aftermarket rims; cat back exhaust; lumpy cam; a driver with spacers listening to Eminem

Ex. *'Did ya see Jaxson bought a new Landscaper's Lambo after his compo claim came through …'*

M1 Mansion

/ ˈɛm-wʌn ˈmænʃən /

1. A Grey Nomad's caravan
2. A small house towed at 95km/h by retired Boomers
3. Transient living quarters spotted on the highways of Australia

Ex. *'Sorry I'm late, I got stuck on the Hume behind an M1 Mansion getting dragged along at a snail's pace …'*

Malaysian Billycart

/ məˈleɪən ˈbɪlikat /

1. A Proton Jumbuck
2. A small half-tonne ute manufactured in Malaysia, featuring not enough grunt to pull the skin off a rice pudding
3. Vehicle used by retired farmers to check the letterbox

See also: The last true automotive deathtrap

Ex. *'Every Sunday, Grandpa scoots into town to pick up the paper in his Malaysian Billycart …'*

AUTOMOTIVE

Marrickville Mercedes

/ ˈmærəkvɪl məˈseɪdiz /

1. A Chrysler Valiant
2. A Winfield-scented sedan, driven by aging Mediterranean hunks from the light industrial suburbs under the flight path
2. A suburban muscle car powered by a straight six-head cylinder engine with triple Weber carburettors

Notes: One of the original 'Big 3' Australian-made vehicles, alongside the Holden Kingswood and the Ford Falcon

Ex. *'I spotted a national treasure at Beaurepaires this morning, a Marrickville Mercedes rolled into the carpark blaring a bit of INXS …'*

Motorcycle Enthusiast

/ ˈmoʊtəsaɪkəl ɛnˈθuziæst /

1. A bikie
2. A member of an outlaw motorcycle club, often covered in tattoos and jacked with Gold Coast–grown muscle

Ex. *'I'd be steering clear of that new bloke at work with the tatts, I hear he's a Motorcycle Enthusiast …'*

Nullarbor Nightrider

/ ˈnʌləbɔ ˈnaɪtraɪdə /

1. An overnight flight from Perth to Sydney
2. A long haul plane ride crossing the Australian continent

Ex. *'I'm flying over to Perth for a wedding next weekend, gotta jump on board the Nullarbor Nightrider …'*

Pious Pious

/ ˈpaɪəs ˈpaɪəs /

1. A Toyota Prius
2. A hybrid electric vehicle with a 1.8-litre petrol engine

Ex. *'My new neighbour Teresa is unbearable, she snots around in her Pious Pious like she's living in 2035 …'*

Ram Raid

/ ˈræm reɪd /

1. A modified Subaru WRX STI
2. A souped-up street rally car with an aftermarket spoiler, rims and doof doof speaker system
3. Preferred vehicle of the suburban drug-dealing hoon or jewellery shop heist criminal

See also: Rexy

Ex. *'My sister's new boyfriend turned up to Easter driving a Ram Raid and Mum's heaps off it …'*

AUTOMOTIVE

Sleeve Tatt Sled

/ ˈsliv tæt ˈslɛd /

1. A jetski
2. A jet-propelled aquatic vehicle, driven for recreation by FIFO workers and Crown Lager enthusiasts
3. Preferred mode of water transport for the people from the Shire or northern Brisbane

Ex. *'Ya hear Jordan just got his finance approved for that Honda R-12X? That bloke can't wait to spend his weekends hooning round on a Sleeve Tatt Sled …'*

Supré Racer

/ supˈreɪ ˌreɪsə /

1. A Suzuki Swift
2. A zippy suburban hatchback, driven by hairdressing apprentices
and local girls who know all the gossip in town

See also: Green P8

Ex. *'I was down the street and spotted Victoria from Illusions Hair
& Beauty doing mainies in her Supré Racer …'*

Geography

Geography

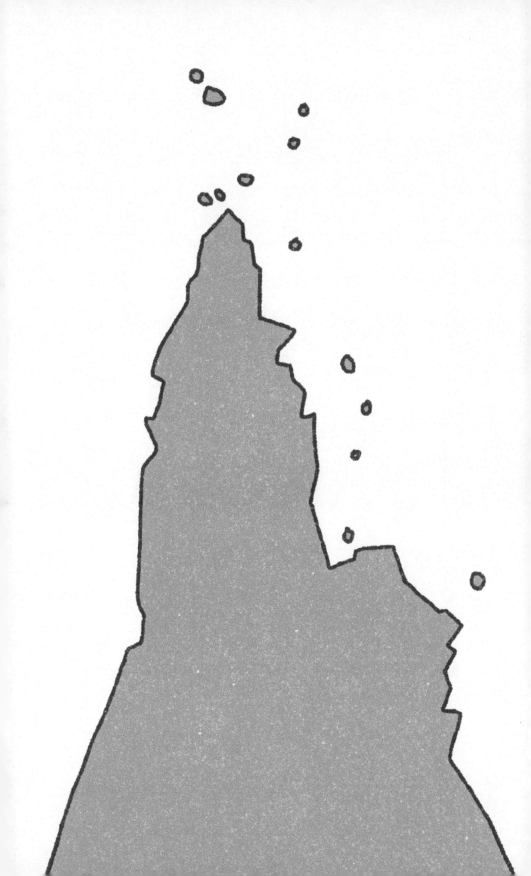

In this section we go around Australia and look at some of the iconic landscapes and human settlements that are worth talking about, which is why it's called 'Geography'.

In previous chapter introductions, I've explained that some terms of reference can be quite disparaging of the place or the person. In this chapter, that statement would also be fairly accurate.

But as you'd know, the most offensive sledges a town can cop come from its own residents. It may be a shithole, but it's our shithole et cetera.

It wasn't until the 1986 release of *Crocodile Dundee* that Australians became confident that our country was beautiful. Dangerous, sure. But beautiful.

It's not clear what exactly Paul Hogan did to change our national psyche, but that scene of Linda Kozlowski crouching next to a picturesque billabong in a Brazilian one-piece swimsuit had to have helped.

Before that, Australians were self-deprecating in the way we spoke about our glorious country. Everyone except the First Nations people, of course – they have a whole culture dedicated to showing great respect for the land, so you can imagine their confusion as to why we would undersell it like that.

There's so much to see, but back then we preferred to write it all off and conform to the British idea that our country was nothing more than a 'backwater colony' – a more humid version of the shittier parts of England.

That's changed though.

Today, we can't get enough of it. Baby Boomers take to the highways like Mad Max in their caravans. We've got millions of Australians opting for sea changes, tree changes and the more climate-focused degree changes.

Finally there's an appreciation of our own backyard. It's a romance that's only been intensified by the closed borders during this pandemic.

Still, we are always prone to giving each other shit. Or giving ourselves shit. So don't get offended by this chapter if we tee off on your hometown.

Arafat

/ ˈærəfæt /

1. Ararat, Victoria
2. A proud rural epicentre in South West Victoria; home to the lesser known Australian Gold Rush and an obesity epidemic that saw them host an entire season of *The Biggest Loser*

Ex. *'Taking the kids down to Arafat this weekend to see their Nan. Things are starting to look up for that town ...'*

Australia's Utah

/ əsˌtreɪljəz ˈjuta /

1. The Hills District, Sydney
2. Australia's Bible Belt, a collection of suburbs in the north west of Sydney renowned for a high density of Hillsong Christians and pyramid scheme participants

Ex. *'Christ, I got stuck sitting in a Pennant Hills traffic jam, took me an age to make it through Australia's Utah ...'*

The Badlands

/ ðə ˈbædlændz /

1. Dubbo, New South Wales
2. Regional city in the central west of NSW, well known for its zoo, sporting celebrities and high crime rate

Ex. *'The boys and I are gearing up for a big roadtrip, we've gotta head out to The Badlands for a touch footy comp next weekend ...'*

Billie Wheeler

/ ˌbɪli ˈwilə /

1. Biloela, Queensland
2. A rural town in central Queensland, located in the Shire of Banana

Ex. *'Heading out to Lake Callide for a fishing trip, it's just a touch outside of Billie Wheeler ...'*

The Buckshot

/ ðə ˈbʌkʃɒt /

1. Coober Pedy
2. The 'Opal Capital of the World', a town in the north of South Australia regarded for a landscape speckled with opal mines and unregistered voters

Ex. *'Stopped off in the Buckshot on our way up to the Alice. She's how I left her ... full of holes.'*

Charlie's Trousers

/ ˌtʃaliz ˈtraʊzəz /

1. Charters Towers
2. A small North Queensland mining town 135km inland from Townsville
3. Notable stronghold of Bob Katter

Ex. *'My cousin Keith is living up in Charlie's Trousers for work, he reckons those boys know how to throw 'em ...'*

The Cement Mill

/ ðə səˈmɛnt mɪl /

1. Great Barrier Reef, Queensland
2. An endangered natural wonder of the world currently at risk of irreparable damage and extinction due to lack of action on climate change

Ex. *'I was up in Mackay the other day just staring out at kilometres of bleached coral, I can see why they call it The Cement Mill ...'*

Equatorial Griffith

/ ɛkwə'tɔriəl 'grɪfəθ /

1. Ingham, North Queensland
2. A small town in Hinchinbrook Shire, renowned for its sugarcane plantations and high density of Italian migrants

See also: New Farm of the North

Ex. *'I'm heading north to go fishing on Hinchinbrook, it's a beaut little island just off the coast of Equatorial Griffith ...'*

Far North Bondi

/ 'fa nɔθ 'bɒndaɪ /

1. Byron Bay, New South Wales
2. A coastal tourist town on the far north coast of NSW

Well known for: Anti-vaxxer-5G-protesting hippies; backpackers; a high invasion of white, wealthy yuppies migrating from Sydney's Bondi Beach

Ex. *'Jenny and the gals flew up to Far North Bondi to visit a yoga retreat for the weekend ...'*

The Garden of Gina

/ ðə 'gadn əv 'dʒinə /

1. The Pilbara, Western Australia
2. The mining region west of Newman, jointly operated by Rio Tinto and Hancock Prospecting

Ex. *'After a three-week swing in The Garden of Gina, Kane caught a taxi directly to the Perth Casino ...'*

God's Country

/ ˈgɒdz ˌkʌntri /

1. Newcastle, New South Wales
2. Harbour city on the east coast of Australia
3. Birthplace of Silverchair and the VCR cocktail

Known for: Queens Wharf punch-ons; wannabe Byron Bay influencers; Donut King franchises

Ex. *'Leavin' the rat race this weekend, gonna shoot up the M1 and sink a few VCRs in God's Country ...'*

The Free State

/ ðə ˈfri steɪt /

1. Adelaide, South Australia
2. The City of Churches, a medium-sized metropolitan area home to 1.3 million Australians who take great pleasure in telling everyone that their city was settled by free people and not convicts

Ex. *'Gotta fly to The Free State for Christmas and visit my weird cousins ...'*

The Front Line

/ ðə ˈfrʌnt laɪn /

1. Inner-north Melbourne, Victoria; the Front Line of urban gentrification
2. A collection of suburbs north of the city of Melbourne, famous as the birthplace of oat-based coffee orders, fixie bicycles and the displacement of housing commission residents

Ex. *'My mate Xavier just moved down to The Front Line, he should fit right in there with his collection of vintage Guns N' Roses t-shirts ...'*

God's Holding Paddock

/ gɒdz ˈhoʊldɪŋ ˌpædək /

1. Buderim, Queensland
2. Urban centre on the Sunshine Coast of Queensland, a region packed with farming retirees and aged care facilities
3. Birthplace of Robert and Bindi Irwin

Ex. *'We've set up Pop in a little duplex out the back of God's Holding Paddock ...'*

The Goon Belt

/ ðə ˈɡʊd bɛlt /

1. Pokolbin, New South Wales
2. The Hunter Valley wine region famous for hosting weddings, hens' weekends and boozy 'wine tasting' bus trips which end with patrons carrying their heels into Cessnock

Ex. *'Nat and the girls had their hens' weekend in The Goon Belt, apparently one of them spewed on the golf course ...'*

The Grimalayas

/ ðə ɡrɪməˈleɪəz /

1. The Blue Mountains, New South Wales
2. A rugged, mountainous region west of Sydney, popular with busloads of tourists and locals who love a punch-on

Ex. *'Came through The Grimalayas on the way back from Bathurst, but the fog was so thick I couldn't even see the Three Sisters ...'*

The Illiterate Isle

/ ðə ɪˈlɪtərət aɪl /

1. Tasmania
2. The island state of Australia, separated by Bass Strait
3. State famous for picturesque landscapes, fresh air and illiteracy

Ex. *'Spent the weekend down in The Illiterate Isle … Tell ya what, lucky no one down there can read some of the shit on the wall at MONA …'*

The Ironing Board

/ ðə ˈaɪənɪŋ bɔd /

1. Hay Plains, New South Wales
2. A place so flat that if ya dog runs away you'll see it run for days
3. One of the flattest places on earth

Ex. *'Went for a drive across The Ironing Board, maybe the earth is flat!? That horizon goes on for years …'*

Irukandji Miami

/ ɪrəˈkændʒi maɪˌæmi /

1. Darwin, Northern Territory
2. Capital city of the Northern Territory, gateway to Kakadu and Litchfield National Park
3. City famous for its all-year-round steamy tropical climate and extremely venomous species of box jellyfish that have prevented the region from becoming a major capital

Ex. *'Taking the kids up to Irukandji Miami for the winter holidays, hoping to see a coupla crocs in the Top End …'*

GEOGRAPHY

Johperth

/ ˈjoʊpɜθ /

1. Perth, Western Australia
2. Capital city of the west, a city known for its tight border restrictions and high rates of South African migrants from the middle class suburbs of Johannesburg

Also known as: Little Pretoria

Ex. *'Had plans to go visit the family in Johperth, but Mark McMao has decided to shut the borders again ...'*

Jonestown

/ ˈdʒoʊnztaʊn /

1. Darling Downs, Queensland
2. Hometown of Alan Jones
3. A plentiful farming region west of Brisbane, often regarded as the food bowl of Queensland

Ex. *'Heading north to visit Coral and Barry, they've got a little intensive cotton operation in Jonestown ...'*

Margaret's Liver

/ ˌmagrəts ˈlɪvə /

1. Margaret River, Western Australia
2. Renowned wine region of WA, synonymous with outdoor weddings, hens' parties and other forms of heavy drinking
3. Filming location of the iconic surfing documentary *The Endless Summer* (1966)

Ex. *'After a big weekend tasting every chardy in Margaret's Liver, Cassie and the girls had a headache for a week ...'*

Neck Nock

/ ˈnɛk nɒk /

1. Cessnock, New South Wales
2. Hunter Valley town famous for mines and wines, the gateway to the Pokolbin wine tasting region
3. Birthplace of The Eighth (Andrew Johns) and home to the Cessnock Goannas Rugby League Football Club

Ex. 'If ya lookin' for the best coal and cabernet in the country, then ya gotta head to Neck Nock, NSW ...'

The Northern Shivers

/ ðə ˌnɔðən ˈʃɪvəz /

1. The Northern Rivers, New South Wales
2. A lush region of pristine beaches, rainforests and prime agricultural land in northern NSW, popular with people who don't vaccinate their kids
3. The area of land stretching from Grafton in the south to Murwillumbah in the north, Kyogle in the west to Ballina in the east

Ex. 'My Aunt Teresa has an eco-friendly mud brick property up in the Northern Shivers where she grows her own crops ... Her kids have constantly got runny noses ...'

Open Sores

/ ˌoʊpən ˈsɔz /

1. Ocean Shores, New South Wales
2. Coastal region in the Northern Rivers, the theological border that separates Byron hippies from Queensland's leather-skinned Boomer retirees and straight-edge teenagers who play in death metal bands

Ex. 'Couldn't get an Airbnb in Byron for Splendour, so we had to stay in a motel in Open Sores ...'

The Red North

/ ðə ˈrɛd nɔθ /

1. The Labor-curious towns of central Queensland
2. A nickname given to the coastline between Central and Far North Queensland, which swings back to voting Labor every eight years or so

Ex. 'Albo might flip The Red North again – they aren't happy with this vaccine roll-out ...'

Shark's Table

/ ˈʃaks ˌteɪbəl /

1. Fremantle, Western Australia
2. Port city located on the mouth of the Swan River, a region renowned for its shark-infested waters

Ex. 'Only the brave swim at South Beach, you'd be lucky not to lose a limb down at Shark's Table ...'

The Steroid Strip

/ ðə ˈstɛrɔɪd strɪp /

1. Gold Coast, Queensland
2. A tourist hotspot on the south coast of Queensland, famous for bikies, trashy nightclubs and the highest rate of botox per capita in Australia
3. Destination of the Schoolies pilgrimage: a once-in-a-lifetime opportunity for school leavers to spew Vodka Cruisers along Cavill Avenue and get bashed by locals

Ex. 'Have you seen Jess from school? She's got a face full of plastic now that she lives on The Steroid Strip ...'

The Tippy Tip

/ ðə ˈtɪpi tɪp /

1. Cape York, Queensland
2. The northernmost peninsula of North Queensland, famous for unspoilt wilderness, adventure tours and pig hunting

Ex. *'Matt and Jesse just took a trip up to The Tippy Tip, should see the pigs they've been shooting ...'*

The Vinegar Belt

/ ðə ˈvɪnəgə bɛlt /

1. Stanthorpe, Queensland
2. The wine region between Tenterfield and Warwick that due to its altitude is known for producing hard-hitting and unusual wines

Ex. *'Was driving through The Vinegar Belt and stopped off to check out the Big Thermometer ...'*

'The'

As an extension of the last chapter, many places around the country can be described in only one word – as long as it's prefixed with 'The'.

They start out simple, like 'The Alice', which hopefully is something I don't need to spell out for you. Or 'The Cape', for that famous Cape at the top of Queensland. Really basic stuff, but it can be lost on someone who's never heard of the place.

Then we slip into something more colloquial like 'The Wok' – which you probably wouldn't know if you weren't familiar with both the topography and climate of Lismore.

At the bottom end of Bundjalung country, this wild town was built inside an old extinct volcano that gets fucking hot in the summer, like a wok.

It also floods a lot in Lismore, and the water doesn't leave The Wok until some old codger from Rotary or the Lions Club does the rounds with a four-stroke Subaru Trash Pump.

When you think about it, a wok kind of looks like the inside of a volcano. So the nickname does make sense.

That's about as complex as it gets, though.

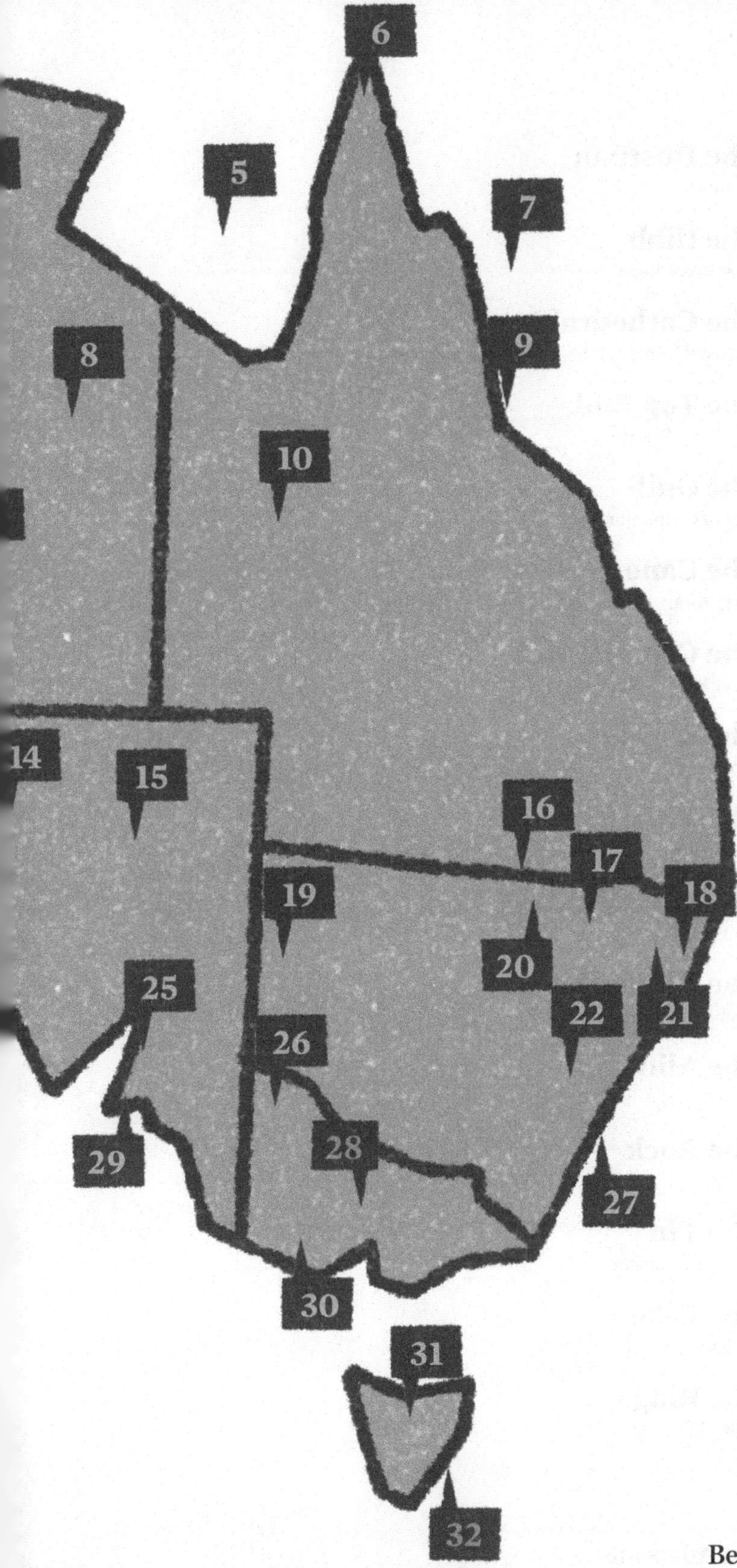

'THE'

1. **The Dustpan**
Broome

2. **The Gibb**
Gibb River Road

3. **The Cathedral**
Cathedral Gorge, Purnululu National Park

4. **The Top End**
Northern Territory

5. **The Gulf**
Gulf of Carpentaria

6. **The Cape**
Cape York

7. **The Cement Mill**
Great Barrier Reef

8. **The Barkley**
Tableland

9. **The Ville**
Townsville

10. **The Isa**
Mount Isa

11. **The Kimberley**
Kimberley Ranges

12. **The Alice**
Alice Springs

13. **The Rock**
Uluru

14. **The Tin**
Wintinna Station

15. **The Lake**
Lake Eyre

16. **The Ridge**
Lightning Ridge

'THE'

17. **The Gun**
Gunnedah

18. **The Northern Shivers**
Northern Rivers

19. **The Hill**
Broken Hill

20. **The Gate**
Walgett

21. **The Wok**
Lismore

22. **The Hunter**
Hunter Valley

23. **The Boxer**
Oxer Lookout

24. **The Bite**
Great Australian Bite

25. **The Free State**
Adelaide

26. **The Dew**
Mildura

27. **The Gong**
Wollongong

28. **The Bend**
Bendigo

29. **The Mortuary**
Coffin Bay

30. **The Rat**
Ballarat

31. **The Lawn**
Launceston

32. **The Glass**
Wineglass Bay

'THE'

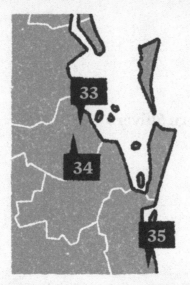

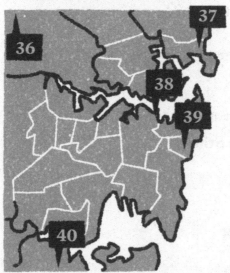

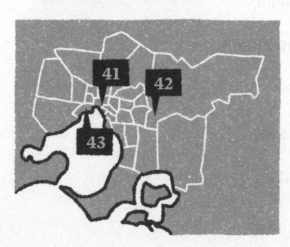

33. The Brown Snake
Brisbane River

34. The Gabba
Brisbane Cricket Ground

35. The Goldie
Gold Coast

36. The Hills
Northwest Sydney

37. The Beaches
Northern Beaches of Sydney

38. The Cross
Kings Cross

39. The East
Eastern suburbs of Sydney

40. The Shire
Southern Shire of Sydney

41. The G
Melbourne Cricket Ground

42. The Patch
Dandenong Ranges

43. The Paris End
Eastern end of Collins Street, Melbourne

'THE'

CHAPTER XII

Rhyming Slang

Australia is one of many nations formed through the bloodshed of British colonialism, so it's no surprise we've been influenced by the poms – more than we care to admit.

Soccer never really took off here, but we did pick up their more problematic cultural traits with both hands. Things like the Westminster system, private schools, rugby, gossip, entitlement, invading the Middle East, and last but not least: binge drinking.

Even the Americans have a very different relationship with alcohol when compared with our two nations. In fact, not many other countries in the world share such an accepted penchant for sitting on your arse all day and drinking tall glasses of brewed cereal grains at an accelerating rate until someone gets either physically hurt or terribly offended.

To this day our tabloid mags still do the best numbers when we have one of those dole-bludging inbreds from the British Royal Family on the front cover.

It seems the only Australians who acknowledge this shameless bootlicking of the monarchy are the blue-bloods who really do wish they were British lords, and act like they are (see: Alexander Downer).

But it's the influence of working-class British culture that Australians seldom acknowledge.

They don't play Rugby League at Oxford, if you know what I'm saying. The Burgess brothers don't sound like any of the kids in *Harry Potter*.

One thing we inherited from these *Billy Elliot* types is rhyming slang.

Initially utilised as a coded dialect that the cops couldn't understand in the East End of London, rhyming slang arrived here with convicts, and then the ten-pound poms after that, permeating its way into Australian vernacular until we had a version of our own.

And our take on Cockney rhyming slang is better. In my opinion anyway. It's kind of like the Euros. Football didn't come home, it went somewhere much nicer. It went to eat squid on the Amalfi Coast. Much the same as rhyming slang. It left East London and came here because it's better here. And every fucking sunburnt pom that came with it will agree.

Babbling Brook

/ ˌbæblɪŋ ˈbrʊk /

1. Cook

Ex. 'You've gotta try the new cutlets on the menu at the Rissole, they've just hired a new Babbling Brook ...'

Bag of Fruit

/ bæg əv ˈfrut /

1. A suit

Ex. 'Got my court hearing on Wednesday, gotta duck down to MJ Bail and pick up a new Bag of Fruit ...'

Barry Crocker

/ ˌbæri ˈkrɒkə /

1. To have a shocker

Ex. 'Dusty missed about six goals on the weekend, he was havin' an absolute Barry Crocker with the boot ...'

Burke & Wills

/ ˈbɜk ənd ˈwɪlz /

1. A bloke who's never worked and never will

Ex. 'Warren's always been a bludging prick, a total Burke & Wills ...'

Bricks and Mortar

/ brɪks ənd ˈmɔtə /

1. Daughter

Ex. 'Heading to the courts to watch the Bricks and Mortar play a bit of tennis ...'

Brown Bread

/ braʊn ˈbrɛd /

1. Dead; to be deceased

Ex. *'Hit a roo on the way back from Coonamble, did the right thing and turned around to check ... but he was well and truly Brown Bread ...'*

Bugs Bunny

/ bʌgz ˈbʌni /

1. Money

Ex. *'Davo never shouts a round, he's so tight with his Bugs Bunny ...'*

Bung Knee

/ bʌŋ ˈni /

1. A bánh mì pork roll

Ex. *'Careful with that place, they like to load up their Bung Knees with lotsa chilli ...'*

Captain Cook

/ ˌkæptən ˈkʊk /

1. A quick look

Ex. *'There's a Commodore for sale down on the highway, might go down and have another Captain Cook ...'*

Cheese 'n' Kisses

/ tʃiz ən ˈkɪsəs /

1. The Missus, a female partner

Ex. *'Nick couldn't stay for a third beer, he had to get home for dinner with the Cheese 'n' Kisses ...'*

Dog's Eye

/ ˈdɒgz aɪ /

1. A meat pie

Ex. *'Got stung at the footy, had to cough up $7.50 for a Dog's Eye and sauce …'*

Elder's Morts

/ ˈɛldəz mɔtz /

1. Shorts

Ex. *'Christ it's freezin' out there, no idea why I wore my Elder's Morts …'*

Fried Rice

/ fraɪd ˈraɪs /

1. Lice, head lice
2. Wingless insects found in the scalp of children/dogs who rarely take a bath

Ex: *'Gotta get some special shampoo for the little fella, he's picked up a bad case of Fried Rice …'*

Harold Holt

/ ˌhærəld ˈhoʊlt /

1. Salt

Ex. *'Hey darl, do you mind passin' the Harold Holt …'*

Joe Blake

/ dʒoʊ ˈbleɪk /

1. Snake

Ex. *'Went for a hike up the mountain and shat my dacks when I came across a big brown Joe Blake ...'*

John Dory

/ dʒɒn ˈdɔri /

1. A story

Ex. *'Danny's been liking a lot of girls' Instagram posts lately, what's the John Dory with him and his missus ...'*

Kevin Sheedy

/ ˌkɛvən ˈʃidi /

1. Seedy after a drink or two

Ex. *'After sinking 16 schooners, Gary woke up feeling a bit Kevin Sheedy ...'*

Kick and Prance

/ kɪk ənd ˈpræns /

1. A dance

Ex. *'Saw Amanda and her friends down at the bowlo having a wild old Kick and Prance ...'*

Kotoni Staggs

/ kə͵toʊni ˈstægz /

1. Bags, Cocaine

Ex. *'You should have seen the line to the toilets at General Admission, must have been a fair few Kotoni Staggs getting around…'*

Miley Cyrus

/ ͵maɪli ˈsaɪrəs /

1. The virus

Ex. *'Raelene was in the city on the weekend, hope she didn't catch that Miley Cyrus…'*

Noah's Ark

/ ͵noʊəz ˈak /

1. A shark

Ex. *'I was having a surf off Ningaloo, swear I spotted a few Noah's Arks out on the reef…'*

Orchestra Stalls

/ ˈɔkəstrə stɔlz /

1. Balls, testicles

See also: The Jatz Crackers (the knackers)

Ex. *'Liam bowled a fast seamer at me and hit me right in the Orchestra Stalls…'*

Pat Malone

/ pæt mə'loʊn /

1. On your own

Ex. *'Saw Robbie hammering the pokies last night on his Pat Malone ...'*

Persian Rugs

/ ˌpɜʒən 'rʌgz /

1. Drugs

Ex. *'Did ya hear Jimmy's been carted off to jail? Got caught selling half a kilo of Persian Rugs ...'*

Ray Martin

/ reɪ 'matn /

1. A carton of beer

See also: A Dolly Parton

Ex. *'Phil stopped by the bottle shop to pick up some smokes and a Ray Martin ...'*

Red Hots

/ rɛd 'hɒts /

1. The Trots, because it's red hot illegal
2. The Harness racing industry

See also: Cheats on Seats, Crims on Rims

Ex. *'My mechanic has a contact down at Menangle, every service he slips me a free tip for the Red Hots ...'*

Ronnie Coote

/ ˌrɒni ˈkut /

1. A root; sexual intercourse

Ex. *'Sandra was on the lookout at the pub, kept telling all her friends she was keen for a Ronnie Coote …'*

Skyrocket

/ ˈskaɪrɒkət /

1. Pocket

Ex. *'Can't for the life of me find my wallet, I swear it was there in my left Skyrocket …'*

Spanish Dancer

/ ˈspænɪʃ ˈdænsə /

1. Cancer

Ex. *'Feeling for old Keith, he's having a tough time – the bloke's been battling his second bout of the Spanish Dancer …'*

Stuart Diver

/ ˌstjuət ˈdaɪvə /

1. Fiver

Ex. *'The Viets down the road will only charge ya a Stuart Diver for a pork roll …'*

Taking a Brad Pitt

/ ˈteɪkɪŋ ə bræd ˈpɪt /

1. Taking a shit

Ex. *'Just heading to the portaloo, gotta take a Brad Pitt …'*

Tea Leaf

/ ˈti lif /

1. A thief

Ex. *'Some Tea Leaf nicked the garden hose from my front yard this morning...'*

Up 'n' Under

/ ʌp ən ˈʌndə /

1. A chunder

Ex. *'Kelly must've have had a raw prawn out on the boat, first thing I heard back at the house was her in the bathroom having an Up 'n' Under ...'*

Betoota Proverbs

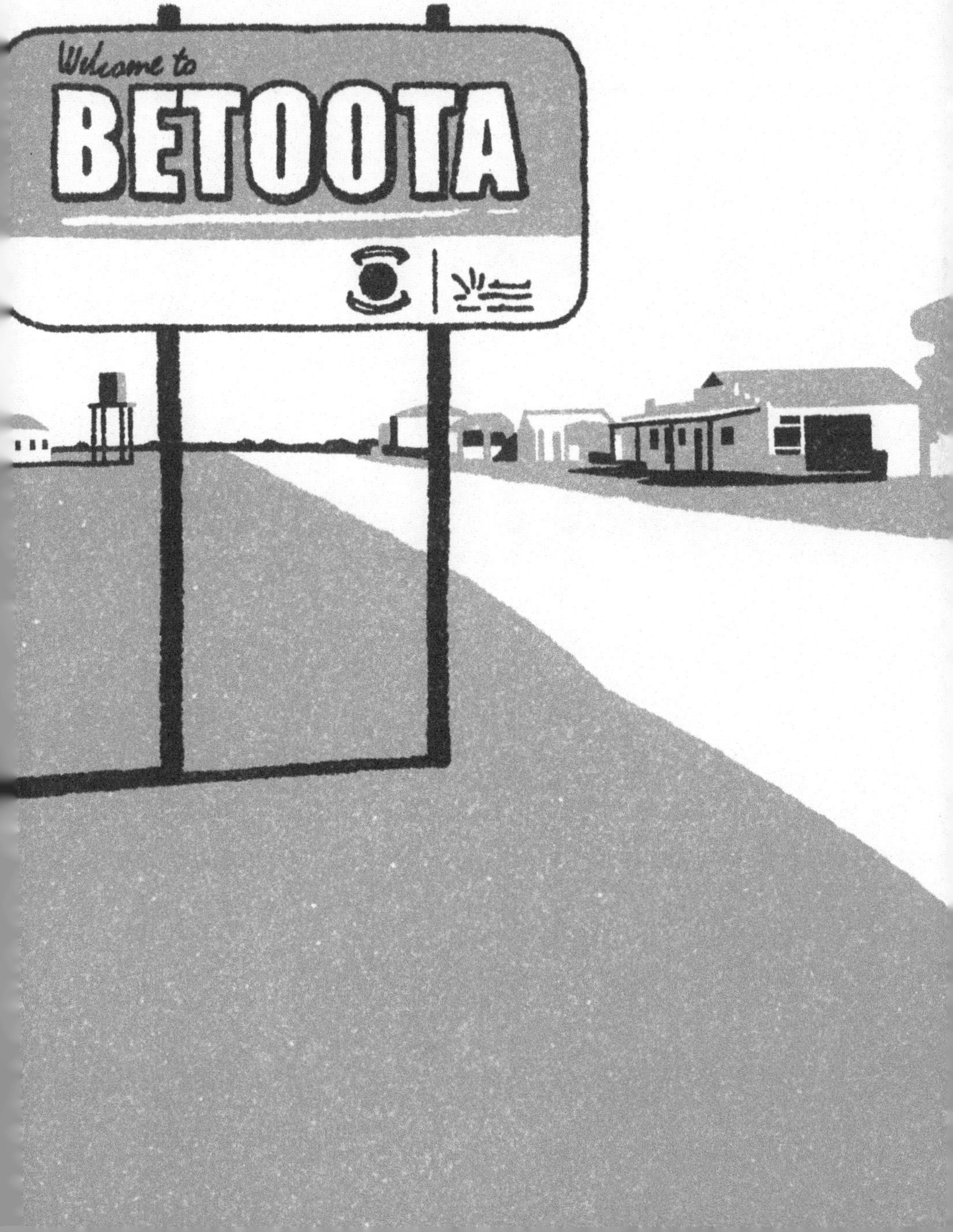
Welcome to
BETOOTA

You've made it to the end of the book, congratulations. This is where we've put the terms that we use regularly here at *The Betoota Advocate*. These are expressions that we employ in lieu of speaking normally, because where's the fun in that.

In my opinion, I think we've saved the best for last.

In this chapter, you'll find proverbs like 'Playing up like a Bali watch', which I think is pretty clever. Not so clever that it's intellectually exclusive, though. You don't need to think too hard to find the humour in it and it's good to cast a wide net with your comedy.

That's what brings people together. A common sentiment. What's the point of pretending to enjoy Wes Anderson films when all you really want to do is mainline some *Flight of the Conchords*.

That's why there's more Australians still listening to *The Twelfth Man* CDs in 2021 than will ever tune into whatever the ABC likes to call light entertainment nowadays.

These proverbs also aren't too red hot, most of them anyway. While snobbery can be the death of conversation, it's equally important to not be exclusively vulgar with your day-to-day parlance.

It's always good to be able to share the same yarn with your nan as you would share with your brother-in-law. There's a time and a place for the sealed section, but it's not good for the soul to only specialise in the dark arts.

Some of these sayings wield a bit more wisdom than others, but they are still fit for a mixed audience.

That's all we try to do with this humble news organ. Something for everyone, and everyone for something.

I think that's a good way to sign off – it sums the book up nicely.

All Hat, No Cattle

/ ɔl ˌhæt noʊ ˈkætl /

1. A person who's all talk and no action
2. A person with a large ego but without substantial achievements

Ex. *'Those Betoota boys are all hat no cattle ...'*

Asparagus

/ əˈspærəgəs /

1. A person who's only good for their (racing) tips
2. A punter who sends around lucrative late mail

Ex. *'That bloke's asparagus, but you wouldn't wanna be stuck in a lift with him ...'*

Awning over the Toyshop

/ ˈɔnɪŋ ˌoʊvə ðə ˈtɔɪʃɒp /

1. A large belly on a man

Ex. *'You can tell Clive hasn't been for a run in a while, bloke's grown a big awning over the toyshop ...'*

Bent Up Like a Half-Shut Pocketknife

/ bɛnt ˌʌp laɪk ə ˌhaf-ʃʌt ˈpɒkətnaɪf /

1. To be in bad physical shape, to have a busted and broken body

Ex. *'Me old man's been shearing sheep his whole life, poor fella is bent up like a half-shut pocketknife ...'*

Better than Lego

/ ˌbɛtə ðæn ˈlɛgoʊ /

1. To acknowledge a euphoric experience
2. A local phrase uttered by Novacastrians to express deep happiness for a situation

Origin: Matty Johns on *Sunrise* after the 1997 Newcastle Knights premiership

Ex. *'Heading up to God's Country to sink Steel City tins and watch the Knights, it'll be better than Lego ...'*

Broken Hill Time

/ ˌbroʊkən ˈhɪl taɪm /

1. To be half an hour late

Origin: In reference to Broken Hill operating on Australian Central Time despite being located in NSW

Ex. *'Cindy is always a bit late, she lives her life on Broken Hill time ...'*

Built like a Butcher's Dog

/ ˌbɪlt laɪk ə ˈbʊtʃəz dɒg /

1. To have a portly build, a heavy frame

Ex. *'Jeez, you can tell Duncan hasn't been to the gym for a while, he's built like a butcher's dog ...'*

Cadbury

/ ˈkædbri /

1. To be easily intoxicated by alcohol, because you can only handle a glass and a half
2. A lightweight, a person who gets drunk on a very small amount of liquor

See also: A Two-Pot Screamer

Ex. *'Never get stuck taking care of Mitch on a night out, there's a reason they call that fella Cadbury …'*

Can Sell Coal to Newcastle

/ kən sɛl ˈkoʊl tə ˈnjukasəl /

1. When someone is very persuasive or convincing
2. An individual with the gift of the gab, a confident speaker

Ex. *'Clint convinced me to stay for another beer, that bloke could sell coal to Newcastle …'*

Champ

/ tʃæmp /

1. A patronising term used to condescend a male counterpart, establish superiority under the guise of friendliness and favour

For feminine uses, see: Sweetie; Honey; Pet

To upsize pronounce: Champ-ioné, Ch-Ümp

Ex. *'Hey mate, are you leaving that parking spot? Yeah sweet as, good onya, champ …'*

Cooked as a Crumpet

/ ˈkʊkt əz ə ˈkrʌmpət /

1. To be suffering from the effects of a large weekend of debaucherous behaviour
2. The outcome of excessive drinking/hedonism

See also: Grog Horrors

Ex. 'After a weekend sinking Jim Beams in Bathurst, I came home on Monday cooked as a crumpet ...'

Couldn't Organise a Rock Fight in a Quarry

/ ˌkʊdənt ˈɔgənaɪz ə ˈrɒk faɪt ɪn ə ˈkwɒri /

1. To describe a person incapable of organising a simple task
2. To be useless, incompetent

Ex. 'Sam forgot to renew his rego, that fella couldn't organise a rock fight in a quarry ...'

Cutting Shapes

/ kʌtɪŋ ˈʃeɪps /

1. To dance, move one's limbs in rhythmic fashion, accompanied by music, beats or tunes
2. To put in a shift at the Arnott's Factory and cut Shapes

Ex. 'Sarah and her rave crew headed out to a bush doof for the weekend, they were cutting shapes from dusk till dawn ...'

Fast Women and Slow Horses

/ fast ˈwɪmən ənd sloʊ ˈhɔsəz /

1. To be broke; to have little to no money due to meaningless romantic flings and gambling

Ex. 'Gotta feel sorry for old Trev, poor bloke has lost all his money on fast women and slow horses ...'

Fatter Than a Broncos Home Crowd

/ ˌfætə ðæn ə ˈbrɒŋkoʊz ˌhoʊm kraʊd /

1. A collective group of portly individuals
2. A gathering of well-padded, large humans

See also: Bob Jane Frame, cos there's a few spare tyres about

Ex. *'My Uncle's had his birthday down at the Sizzler, tell ya everyone was fatter than a Broncos home crowd ...'*

Fits in Like a Violin in a Marching Band

/ fɪts ˈɪn laɪk ə vaɪəˈlɪn ɪn ə ˈmatʃɪŋ bænd /

1. To not match with the surroundings, to not fit in

Ex. *'My brother's new girlfriend is a vegetarian, to be honest she fits into our family like a violin in a marching band ...'*

Good for the Run

/ ˈgʊd fɔ ðə ˈrʌn /

1. To see a positive of a bad result, like a horse trainer claiming their horse running last did good for the run
2. To remain chipper after being badly beaten in sports

Ex. *'First game of the year and we got flogged by 50; besides that it was good for the run ...'*

Hasn't Seen Blue Lately

/ ˌhæzənt sin ˈblu ˌleɪtli /

1. When a man hasn't had a shave in a while
2. When a male hasn't used the blue Gillette razor in a few weeks

Ex. *'Thought Hamo was looking a bit scruffy, he sure hasn't seen blue lately ...'*

It's Not Always the Cowboy That Rides Away

/ ɪts nɒt ˈɔlweɪz ðə ˈkaʊbɔɪ ðæt rʌnz əˈweɪ /

1. When a man's wife leaves him
2. When a female is the instigator in a relationship breakup

Ex. *'Heard that Deborah finally left Wayne for another bloke. These flakey blokes don't realise it's not always the cowboy that rides away ...'*

No Work in Bourke, Fuck all in Blackall

/ noʊ ˈwɜk ɪn ˈbɜk, fʌk ˈɔl ɪn ˈblækɔl /

1. A term used to describe a sub-optimal job market

Ex. *'Two months I've been sniffing round for a job, but there's no work in Bourke, fuck all in Blackall ...'*

On the Chain

/ ɒn ðə ˈtʃeɪn /

1. Shearing slang for having the lowest score

Ex. *'Got bowled out on four, so yeah I'm dirty 'bout being on the chain ...'*

On the Swipes

/ ɒn ðə ˈswaɪpz /

1. To use an online dating application in search of love or a potential partner
2. The act of using a mobile device to improve one's dating life

See also: Fumble on the Bumble; Online Lazy Susie; Lightin' the Tinder Box

Ex. 'Did ya hear Cameron has a new lady friend? He met her over WiFi while he was on the swipes ...'

Playing Up Like a Bali Watch

/ ˌpleɪɪŋ ˈʌp laɪk ə ˈbali wɪtʃ /

1. To be up to mischief; getting into trouble
2. To be acting up like a loose unit

Ex. 'Logan got us kicked out of Cloudland on Saturday night. As usual he was playing up like a Bali watch ...'

Rough as Hessian Undies

/ ˈrʌf əz ˌhɛʃən ˈʌndiz /

1. To be lacking in refinement or sophistication
2. To display limited manners or politeness

See also: Rough as a Sandpaper Thong

Ex. 'The new neighbours have moved in next door. Tell ya what, they're rough as hessian undies ...'

Rung the Shed

/ ˈrʌŋ ðə ʃɛd /

1. To have the highest score

Origin: To have the highest tally in the shearing shed

Ex. 'Brenno was on fire at golf today, he rung the shed on all of us ...'

Sharp as a Bowling Ball

/ 'ʃap əz ə 'boʊlɪŋ bɔl /

1. To lack intelligence or interpersonal skills
2. To appear dimwitted; a little stupid with no spark

See also: A Few Sandwiches Short of a Picnic

Ex. *'That new apprentice is a bit dim, he's about as sharp as a bowling ball …'*

Slower than a Boomer with a QR Code

/ 'sloʊə ðæn ə 'bumə wɪθ ə kju 'a koʊd /

1. To undertake a task slowly and with confusion
2. To fumble over a chore

Ex. *'Got stuck behind a caravan on the freeway, thing was going slower than a Boomer with a QR code …'*

Sooking Like a Blue-Haired Yuppie

/ 'sʊkɪŋ laɪk ə 'blu-hɛəd ˌjʌpi /

1. To have a loud whinge; to continuously complain

Ex. *'Some Karen was having a go at the waiter for the slow service, she was sooking like a blue-haired yuppie …'*

Toey as a Roman Sandal

/ 'toʊi əz ə 'roʊmən ˌsændl /

1. To be sexually aroused, lustful
2. To be on the lookout for sexual activity

Ex. *'After a three-month dry spell, Blake was toey as a Roman sandal …'*

Useful as an Ashtray on a Motorbike

/ ˈjusfəl əz ˈən ˈæʃtreɪ ɒn ə ˈmoʊtəbaɪk /

1. When a device or appliance is broken, unable to be used for its purpose

Ex. 'My Craptiva has blown its head gasket, damn thing is about as useful as an ashtray on a motorbike …'

Walking on Lego

/ ˈwɔkɪŋ ɒn ˈlɛɡoʊ /

1. To be dating someone who has a child/children from a previous relationship
2. To be parenting children not biologically related to oneself

Ex. 'Heard Bailey has got himself a new misso, apparently he's in way over his head walking on Lego …'

Was Your Father a Glass Maker?

/ wəz jɔ ˌfaðə ə ˈɡlasmeɪkə /

1. A term used when someone stands in front of you, obstructing your view
2. Commonly used in pubs when someone is blocking the big screen

Ex. 'Oi mate, was your father a glass maker? Get out of the way …'

What's in Ya Pocket?

/ wɒts ɪn jə ˈpɒkət /

1. An expression screamed at referees by fans pleading for a yellow card
2. Heard every Saturday afternoon at local football ovals

Ex. 'Fuck! That was a high shot – WHAT'S IN YA POCKET, REF?!!'

Wouldn't Take 'Em Fishing

/ ˌwʊdənt ˈteɪk əm ˈfɪʃɪn /

1. To describe a person who's bad company

Ex. *'Yeah Scotty From Marketing is a nice enough bloke – but tell ya what, you wouldn't take him fishing ...'*

Index of Terms

1st Gen Footy 104
365ers 74
Acca Dacca 30
Accountant, the 114
Adelaide 181
Adult Babysitter 44
AirPod with Legs 44
Albury All-Star, the 114
Aldi Alan 16
Alexander the Great 115
Alice Springs 180
Alice, the 180
All Hat, No Cattle 200
American Netball 104
Amex Breakfast 74
Arafat 164
Art Gallery Valerie 45
Asparagus 200
AstroZucchini 6
Australia's Utah 164
Australian Dream, the 152
Aviary 136
Awning over the Toyshop 200
Babbling Brook 188
Bachelor's Handbag 74
Badlands, the 164
Bag of Fruit 188
Bala Pat 115
Bali Bonds 60
Ballarat 181
Bam Bam 115

Bangkok Happy Meal 75
Banglops 152
Barina Brekky 75
Barkley, the 180
Baroness of Broadbeach, the 30
Barry Crocker 188
Barty Party 116
BCF Jeff 45
Beaches, the 183
Bean Counter 46
Becky 46
Beep Tester, the 46
Bend, the 181
Bendigo 181
Bent Up Like a Half-Shut
    Pocketknife 200
Bert Newton 86
Better than Lego 201
Big Blue Bin, the 136
Big Hooah 104
Big Tuna 116
Billie Wheeler 164
Binga 116
Bite, the 181
Black Doctor 75
Black Rat 86
Blue Bloods, the 47
Blue Rocket 87
Bogan Silks 105
Bolt-Ons 60
Boomer Remover 6

Boon Broom 60
Booze Buffet 87
Boozy Balkan, the 31
Boxer, the 181
Brain Varnish 87
Brickie's Brunch 76
Brickie's Laptop 88
Bricks and Mortar 188
Brisbane Cricket Ground 183
Brisbane River 183
Broken Hill 181
Broken Hill Time 201
Broome 180
Brown Bread 189
Brown Snake, the 183
Bruce's Wet Dream 117
Buckshot, the 165
Bugs Bunny 189
Built like a Butcher's Dog 201
Bung Knee 189
Burke & Wills 188
Bush Uce 47
Busted Cocky 47
Byron Bulldozer 152
Byron Nappy 61
Caboolture Crooner 31
Cadbury 202
Caltex Canapé 76
Camperdown Frown, the 16
Can Sell Coal to Newcastle 202
Canberra Conveyor Belt 136
Cancer Shop 137
Cape York 180
Cape, the 180
Captain Cook 189
Cardboardéaux 88
Cathedral Gorge, Purnululu National
    Park 180
Cathedral, the 180
Cattle Tick 137
Cattledog 105
Caxton Street Car Bomb 88
Cement Mill, the 165, 180
Champ 202
Charlie's Trousers 165

Cheese 'n' Kisses 189
Chinese Breath Mints 76
Chippy's Pantry 137
Choppercore 61
Chozzie 77
Christian Cocaine 89
Christmas Cake, the 31
Clog Wog 137
Clown School 138
Coffin Bay 181
Colourful Racing Identity 48
Concrete Cowboy 48
Concreter's Caviar 77
Cooked as a Crumpet 203
Coota Suit 61
Couldn't Organise a Rock Fight in a
    Quarry 203
Country Town Cardashian 49
Covid Coward 6
Covid Refugee 7
Coward's Cordial 89
Craptiva 153
Crims on Rims 89
Cross, the 183
Cul-De-Sacs 62
Curtain Shop 138
Cutting Shapes 203
Dandenong Ranges 183
Darlo Breadline 77
Dead Centre of Town 138
Devil Dodger 49
Dew, the 181
Dictator Dan 16
Digital Durry 90
DINKs 49
Dishlickers 90
Dizzy 117
Dog's Eye 190
Double Parked 90
Double-Barrelled Brigade 17
Drive-Thru Brain Tickle 7
Dubbo Dinner Jacket 62
Duchess of Dalby, the 32
Dunny Door 153
Dustpan, the 180

INDEX OF TERMS

East, the 183
Eastern end of Collins Street,
    Melbourne 183
Eastern suburbs of Sydney 183
EB Games Moustache 62
Eighth, the 117
Elder's Morts 190
Equatorial Griffith 166
Everywhere Eddie 32
Family Court 123
Far North Bondi 166
Fast Women and Slow Horses 203
Fatter Than a Broncos Home
    Crowd 204
Fax Machine 91
Final Word, the 32
Finger, the 33
Fitness Thirst Pants 63
Fits in Like a Violin in a Marching
    Band 204
Floating GOAT, the 118
Flog Clogs 63
Flying Doormat, the 118
Foil Packet Chef, the 33
Foot Falcon 153
Fortunate Sons 17
Four-Legged Lottery 105
Free State, the 167, 181
Frenzal Ropes 63
Fried Rice 190
Front Line, the 167
Fun Freezer, the 33
Functional Alcoholism 106
Funky 118
G, the 183
Gabba, the 183
Garden of Gina, the 166
Garrrrrry 119
Gate, the 181
Gatorade Saxophone 91
Gibb River Road 180
Gibb, the 180
Glass Mask 7
Glass, the 181
God 119

God's Country 167
God's Holding Paddock 168
Gold Coast 183
Goldie, the 183
Gong, the 181
Good for the Run 204
Goon Belt, the 168
Grain-Fed Mullet 64
Grandma's Carpark 139
Grandpa Kev 17
Gravy Day 139
Great Australian Bite 181
Great Barrier Reef 180
Greek Broom 139
Greeks, the 140
Grimalayas, the 168
Grog Horrors 91
Guangzhou Go-Kart 154
Gulf of Carpentaria 180
Gulf, the 180
Gun, the 34
Gun, the 181
Gunnedah 181
Harold Holt 190
Hasn't Seen Blue Lately 204
He Who Shall Not Be Prime
    Minister 18
Helmet 119
Her Majesty's Hotel 140
Hermit Park Handshake 92
High Horse 154
Higher-Vis Education 141
Highway Hilton 141
Hill, the 181
Hills, the 183
Hinch's Hermès 92
Honey Badger 120
Hot Laps 154
Hot Mess Gladys 18
Hungry Jackboots 64
Hunter Valley 181
Hunter, the 181
Hydraulic 50
Illiterate Isle, the 169
Indian Itchy Lung 8

Irish Twins 50
Ironing Board, the 169
Irukandji Miami 169
Isa, the 180
It's Not Always the Cowboy That Rides
   Away 205
Jesus Jandals 64
Jingles 120
Joe Blake 191
JohAnna 19
John Dory 191
Johperth 170
Jonestown 170
Juke Box 50
Kaftan Diesel 92
Kalyn the Alien 120
Karen 51
Kawasaki King 51
Keith's Arrow 34
Kevin Sheedy 191
Keyhole Ball 106
Kick and Prance 191
Kimberley Ranges 180
Kimberley, the 180
King of the North, the 121
Kings Cross 183
Knock Shop 141
Koori Rose, the 35
Korea 121
Kotoni Staggs 192
Kremlin, the 19
Kyng Kyrgios 121
Lake Eyre 180
Lake, the 180
Landscaper's Lambo 155
Last Good Catholics, the 142
Last Resort, the 142
Launceston 181
Lawn, the 181
Leftie Factory 142
Ley Ley 122
Lightning 52
Lightning Ridge 180
Linenfluencer 52
Lismore 181

London Fog 52
Long Drop, the 140
M1 Mansion 155
Mackay Yoga 93
Mad Katter 19
Madame Butterfly 122
MAFS Mouth 65
Malaysian Billycart 155
Margaret's Liver 170
Marilyn Hanson 20
Mark McMao 20
Marrickville Mercedes 156
Melbourne Cricket Ground 183
Member for Manila, the 21
Mensa Club, the 143
Michelle Pfeiffer 8
Mildura 181
Miley Cyrus 192
Milk, the 106
Milton Mango 93
MJ Bail 65
Moreton Bay Porridge 78
Mortuary, the 181
Mosman Gumboots 65
Motorcycle Enthusiast 156
Mount Isa 180
Mr TikTok 123
Mungo 107
Nasal Appraisal 8
National Sport, the 107
Neck Nock 171
Neutron Bomb, the 35
News, the 35
No Work in Bourke, Fuck all in
   Blackall 205
Noah's Ark 192
Nobody 123
Northern Beaches of Sydney 183
Northern Rivers 181
Northern Shivers, the 171, 181
Northern Territory 180
Northwest Sydney 183
Nose Beers 93
Nullarbor Nightrider 156
Nut Trucker 108

INDEX OF TERMS

Old Mate Out Front 94
Old Pom, the 143
On the Chain 205
On the Swipes 206
One Eyed Blue, the 124
Open Sores 171
Orchestra Stalls 192
Our Geoffrey 36
Oxer Lookout 181
Paddington Tankwater 78
Paid Leave Porter 21
Pangolin's Kiss 8
Paris End, the 183
Pat Malone 193
Patagonia Parade 9
Patch, the 183
Pavement Sprayer 78
Pensioner's Playground 143
Persian Rugs 193
Pez 124
Pfizer Chief 9
Pied Piper, the 21
Pigeon 124
Pinger Polo 66
Pious Pious 157
Plague Enthusiast 9
Playing Up Like a Bali Watch 206
Plumber's Picnic 79
Private School Pluggers 66
Pub with No Beer 144
Puberty Perfume 66
Punter 125
Put on a Spider 94
Pymble Pirate, the 36
Queen Street Mullet 67
Queen, the 125
Raging Bull, a 86
Raging Bull, the 125
Rah Rah 108
Ram Raid 157
Rat, the 181
Rat's Coffin 79
Ray Martin 193
Recedes-Benz 67
Red Hots 193

Red North, the 172
Ridge, the 180
Rissole 144
Riverina Rollie 94
Rock, the 180
Rocket Rod 126
Rolling Sizzler 79
Ronnie Coote 194
Rough as Hessian Undies 206
Rough Riding 108
RSL Tan, the 22
Rumour Mill 144
Rung the Shed 206
Rural Networking 109
Russian Handball 95
Rusty Rabbit, the 36
Schooey Schooey Moi Moi 95
School Shooter 67
School Zone 145
Schooner Shop 145
Scientologist 53
Scomo Showbag 10
Scotty from Marketing 22
Shanghai Sam 23
Shark's Table 172
Sharon Woods 126
Sharp as a Bowling Ball 207
Shire, the 183
Silverhair 37
Skippy 127
Skull 126
Skyrocket 194
Sleeve Tatt Sled 157
Slower than a Boomer with a QR
    Code 207
SOCK 53
Soggy Blocks 80
Son of God 127
Sooking Like a Blue-Haired Yuppie 207
Southern Shire of Sydney 183
Spag Bol 127
Spanish Dancer 194
Speaking Greek 95
Speed Dealers 68
Spice Girls 10

Sponsored Continental 80
Steroid Strip, the 172
Sticky Lid 68
Stonefruit Smoothie 96
Stuart Diver 194
Stunner from Gunner, the 37
Sugarcane Champagne 96
Sunburnt Sudoku 145
Supré Racer 158
Swing Voter 53
Sydney Sneeze 10
Tableland 180
Taking a Brad Pitt 194
Talisman of the Top End 37
Taree Ferrari, the 128
Tasmanian Toiga 23
Tea Leaf 195
Terminator, the 24
Terminator, the 128
Terry Tough Cunt 54
Test Match 128
That Bald Prick 30
Thorpedo 129
Three One 54
Throat, the 129
Tin, the 180
Tippy Tip, the 173
Todd Carney Cottees 96
Toey as a Roman Sandal 207
Tommy Turbo 129
Tongan Thor 130
Toowoomba Pumba, the 130
Top End, the 180
Town Crier 38
Townsville 180
Townsville Sunrise 97
Trophy Hunter, the 38
Trough, the 146

Truckie's Toothpaste 97
Trustafarian 55
Tuesday Frisbee 80
Tupperware Christian 55
Uluru 180
Uncle Tony X 24
Up 'n' Under 195
Useful as an Ashtray on a
    Motorbike 208
VCR 97
Vertical Consumption 11
Victor Bravo 98
Victor the Inflictor 130
Victorian Leg Tennis 109
Viets, the 146
Ville, the 180
Vinegar Belt, the 173
Voice, the 131
Walgett 181
Walking on Lego 208
Wall of Knowledge, the 146
Waltzing Matt Hilder 131
Wanker's Waistcoat 68
Was Your Father a Glass Maker? 208
Water Torture 109
Weber Wheels 69
What's in Ya Pocket? 208
Whistle, the 38
White Eggs 98
White White 147
Wick Wilkins, the 39
Wineglass Bay 181
Wintinna Station 180
Wizard, the 131
Wok, the 181
Wollongong 181
Wouldn't Take 'Em Fishing 209
Zoo, the 147